Grammar and Writing 5

Teacher Packet

Answer Keys and Tests

First Edition

Christie Curtis

Mary Hake

Houghton Mifflin Harcourt Publishers, Inc.

Grammar and Writing 5

First Edition

Teacher Packet
Answer Keys and Tests

ISBN-13: 978-1-4190-9849-9
ISBN-10:   1-4190-9849-7

Houghton Mifflin Harcourt Publishers, Inc.
181 Ballardvale Street
Wilmington, MA 01887

http://saxonhomeschool.com

Printed in the United States of America.

1 2 3 4 5 6 7 8 862 16 15 14 13 12 11 10 09

Writing 5 Table of Contents

Fifth Grade Grammar & Writing Schedule

iv

School Day	Grammar Lesson	Writing Lesson	School Day	Grammar Lesson	Writing Lesson	School Day	Grammar Lesson	Writing Lesson
1	1		49	test 7	9	97		22
2	2		50	41		98		23
3	3		51	42		99	76	
4	4		52	43		100	77	
5	5		53	44		101	78	
6	6		54	45		102	79	
7	7		55	test 8	10	103	80	
8	8		56	46		104	test 15	24
9	9		57	47		105		25
10	10		58	48		106		26
11	test 1	1	59	49		107		
12	11		60	50		108	81	
13	12		61	test 9	11	109	82	
14	13		62		12	110	83	
15	14		63	51		111	84	
16	15		64	52		112	85	
17	test 2	2	65	53		113	test 16	27
18		3	66	54		114	86	
19		4	67	55		115	87	
20	16		68	test 10	13	116	88	
21	17		69	56		117	89	
22	18		70	57		118	90	
23	19		71	58		119	test 17	28
24	20		72	59		120		29
25	test 3	5	73	60		121		30
26	21		74	test 11	14	122	91	
27	22		75		15	123	92	
28	23		76		16	124	93	
29	24		77	61		125	94	
30	25		78	62		126	95	
31	test 4	6	79	63		127	test 18	31
32	26		80	64		128	96	
33	27		81	65		129	97	
34	28		82	test 12	17	130	98	
35	29		83	66		131	99	
36	30		84	67		132	100	
37	test 5	7	85	68		133	test 19	
38	31		86	69		134	101	
39	32		87	70		135	102	
40	33		88	test 13	18	136	103	
41	34		89		19	137	104	
42	35		90		20	138	105	
43	test 6	8	91	71		139	test 20	
44	36		92	72		140	106	
45	37		93	73		141	107	
46	38		94	74		142	108	
47	39		95	75		143	109	
48	40		96	test 14	21	144	110...	

Topical Table of Contents

Sentence Structure

Eight Parts of Speech

Verbs

Nouns

Pronouns

Adjectives

Prepositions

Adverbs

Conjunctions

Interjections

Usage

Spelling Rules

Diagramming

Writing Lessons

WRITING LESSON 1   The Sentence

a. My neighbor Jalana has a vegetable garden.

b. She grows squash, tomatoes, and beans.

c. That ripe tomato will taste delicious.

d. The question confused them.

e. The loud noise had startled Max.

f. A dump truck made the loud noise.

WRITING LESSON 2   The Paragraph

a. Peter is an artist!

b. People call Michigan the Great Lake State for good reasons.

c. Last night's windstorm made a big mess.

d. ~~My cousin rides horses.~~

e. ~~My friend Jenny used to live on an island.~~

f. ~~Lemons and oranges are citrus fruits.~~

g. That bright star is far away.

h. We can identify stars and planets.

i. Saturn's rings fascinated Jo.

j. Most people appreciate Sergio's humor.

WRITING LESSON 3   The Paragraph, Part 2

a. 3, 4, 1, 2

b. *Each student will write his or her paragraph on the lines provided or on a separate sheet of paper that can be turned in to the teacher.*

c. The Gem State is a fitting nickname for Idaho.

d. ~~Nancy's house is yellow with white trim.~~

e. June has short, curly hair. (or) June's hair is short and curly.

f. Eagles soar and land in high places.

g. Rufus's barking distracted Debby.

h. All the tourists can see the magnificent statue.

WRITING LESSON 4   The Paragraph, Part 3

a. 3, 5, 1, 4, 2

b. *Students' questions will vary. Each student will write his or her paragraph on the lines provided or on a separate sheet of paper that can be turned in to the teacher.*

c. Andrew collects seashells.

d. ~~Elle has a hamster named Trina.~~

e. Elle has a neat, clean desk.

f. We drove through Colorado, Kansas, and Missouri

g. The gift surprised me.

h. Rufus might frighten Max's cat.

Additional Practice: *Each student will write his or her paragraph on a sheet of paper.*

WRITING LESSON 5   The Essay: Three Main Parts

a. 1, 4, 3, 2

b. *Students' paragraphs will vary.*

c. The Austrian Franz Schubert became a famous music composer.

d. ~~Ting has a bird and two fish.~~

e. Juan has a huge, long-haired cat.

f. Ms. Hoo has lived in North Dakota, Minnesota, and New York.

g. The dog's barking might have startled the horse.

h. Schubert composed that waltz.

i. Introductory Paragraph
Body Paragraph
Body Paragraph
Body Paragraph
Concluding Paragraph

WRITING LESSON 6   The Essay: Introductory Paragraph

a. <u>Three of the most famous German composers are Johann Sebastian Bach, Felix Mendelssohn, and Robert Schumann.</u>

b. 1, 3, 4, 2

c. *Students' paragraphs will vary.*

d. <u>This spring I shall plant a vegetable garden.</u>

e. ~~Mr. Shade wears red tennis shoes.~~

f. The Komodo dragon has a long, forked tongue.

g. My classmate Juan plays the violin and the cello.

h. Aunt Steph baked that apple pie.

i. Introductory (Paragraph)
1. Introductory sentence
2. Thesis statement
Body (Paragraph)
Body (Paragraph)
Body (Paragraph)
Concluding (Paragraph)

WRITING LESSON 7   The Essay: Body Paragraph

a. *Students may use the lines provided or a separate sheet of paper to be handed to the teacher.*

b. *See student work.*

c. <u>I like the desert's creatures, the wide open space, and the hot temperatures.</u>

d. 2, 1, 4, 3

e. <u>Alaska is the source of many products that people in other states enjoy.</u>

f. ~~Daniela collects postage stamps.~~

g. The hens laid six big brown eggs.

h. My cousin John plays the guitar.

i. Ron and Susan peel the potatoes.

j. *See chart showing structure of typical five-paragraph essay.*

WRITING LESSON 8   The Essay: Concluding Paragraph

a. *Students may use the lines provided or a separate sheet of paper.*

b. <u>We all can make changes for the better in our lifestyles.</u>

c. 2, 4, 1, 3

d. <u>Norman feels irritable today.</u>

e. ~~Pigeons come in many colors.~~

f. Dr. Ledfoot drives a small red truck.

g. Lucy has straight brown hair.

h. Machines assemble these toys.

i. Introductory Paragraph
   1. Introductory Sentence
   2. Thesis Statement
Body Paragraph
   Topic sentence
   1. Supporting sentence
   2. Supporting sentence
   3. Supporting sentence
Body Paragraph
   Topic sentence
   1. Supporting sentence
   2. Supporting sentence
   3. Supporting sentence
Body Paragraph
   Topic sentence
   1. Supporting sentence
   2. Supporting sentence
   3. Supporting sentence
Concluding Paragraph
   1. Restatement of thesis
   2. Reference to each topic sentence
   3. Clincher sentence

WRITING LESSON 9 — The Essay: Transitions

a. also

b. Besides that

c. therefore

d. I believe that we should keep the pigeons because of their beauty, their friendliness, and their pleasant cooing sounds.

e. 2, 1, 3, 4

f. James loves to photograph wildlife.

g. ~~Denver is the capital of Colorado.~~

h. Ted wrote a long, funny essay.

i. Gia has a turtle named Oliver.

j. Moths destroyed my wool coat.

k. *See chart showing structure of typical five-paragraph essay.*

WRITING LESSON 10 — Brainstorming for Ideas

Students may use the lines provided or a separate sheet of paper to be handed to the teacher.

a. Furthermore

b. on the other hand

c. similarly

d. Kurt is learning to sketch animals.

e. ~~Corn grows in Iowa.~~

f. The finch had a red head and a black beak.

g. Ms. Hoo is wearing large, round sunglasses.

h. The young artist sketched various reptiles.

i. *See chart showing structure of typical five-paragraph essay.*

WRITING LESSON 11 — Writing a Complete Essay

See student work.

WRITING LESSON 12 — Evaluating your Essay

See student work.

Note: *Some teachers will prefer that their students use a 1-5 number scale instead of yes/no on the evaluation forms.*

Example:
5 = excellent
4 = good
3 = satisfactory
2 = needs improvement
1 = poor

When the student can write a 4 or 5 on each blank, then his or her essay is complete.

WRITING LESSON 13 — Supporting a Topic Sentence with Experiences, Examples, Facts, and Opinions

a. *Students may use the lines provided or a separate sheet of paper to be handed to the teacher.*

b. First

c. as a result

d. Therefore

e. Nels captures the attention of many creatures at the lake.

f. ~~Caribou roam the plains of Alaska.~~

g. Tyrell wrote me a long, newsy letter.

h. The hungry black bears eat fish and wild berries.

i. Nels fed the turtles.

j. *See chart showing structure of typical five-paragraph essay.*

Grammar & Writing Textbook

LESSON 1   The Sentence: Two Parts

Practice 1

a. The United States

b. The city of Montgomery

c. measures 52,432 square miles

d. comprises 50,750 square miles

e. Water | covers 1673 square miles in Alabama.

f. Tyrell and Marisol | live in Alabama

g. essential

h. nonessential

Review Set 1

1. essential

2. Nonessential

3. essential

4. two

5. subject

6. predicate

7. sentence

8. predicate

9. Farmers

10. Poultry and eggs

11. Lumber and wood products

12. Alabama's flag

13. resembles a Confederate Battle Flag

14. is the yellowhammer

15. belongs to the woodpecker family

16. border Alabama

17. Booker T. Washington | founded a school in Tuskegee, Alabama.

18. Boll weevils | destroyed a cotton crop!

19. George Washington Carver | experimented with peanuts and other crops.

20. Julian | made a peanut butter pie.

21. Sweet potato pie | is my favorite.

22. Tyrone's chickens | laid two dozen eggs!

23. His rooster | crows too early.

24. Miss Snoot | complains.

25. She | wakes in a bad mood.

LESSON 2   Four Types of Sentences

Practice 2

a. interrogative

b. exclamatory

c. declarative

d. imperative

e. synonyms

f. antonyms

Review Set 2

1. Essential

2. antonym

3. declarative

4. interrogative

5. imperative

6. exclamatory

7. period

8. subject

9. predicate

10. capital

11. question mark

12. exclamation point

13. declarative

14. exclamatory

15. interrogative

16. declarative
17. imperative
18. The willow ptarmigan
19. seafood
20. Moose and brown bears
21. The economy
22. Petroleum and natural gas
23. adopted a state flag in 1959
24. represents the sky, the sea, the lakes, and the wildflowers
25. contains seven stars
26. connect Juneau to the rest of the world
27. The salmon swam upstream.
28. Where is Mount McKinley?
29. Alaska's motto | is "North to the Future."
30. People | rushed to the goldfields.

LESSON 3 Simple Subjects • Simple Predicates

Practice 3

a. caves
b. states
c. roadrunner
d. raise
e. displays
f. formed
g. scarce
h. abundant

Review Set 3

1. subject
2. subject
3. predicate
4. verb

5. subject
6. Nonessential
7. plentiful
8. synonyms
9. antonyms
10. Antonyms
11. Mount McKinley
12. United States
13. Mount Katmai
14. glacier
15. live
16. lies
17. are blooming
18. has been following
19. Prospectors discovered gold.
20. Why is Wyatt Earp famous?
21. Look out for the snake!
22. Watch where you step.
23. imperative
24. interrogative
25. declarative
26. exclamatory
27. The river | eroded the soil.
28. Many tourists | have walked through this ghost town.
29. Coyotes | are howling at the moon.
30. Spanish explorers | were searching for "Cities of Gold."

LESSON 4 Reversed Subject and Predicate Split Predicate

Practice 4

a. pessimism
b. optimism

c. ladybugs

d. gopher

e. Have migrated

f. Did Hear

More Practice 4   *See Master Worksheets*
Teachers: "More Practice" is optional.
Some students will need it; others will not.

Review Set 4

1. predicate
2. subject
3. verb
4. action
5. sentence
6. essential
7. Scarce
8. antonyms
9. synonyms
10. Synonyms
11. Arkansans
12. mockingbird
13. blossoms
14. William J. Clinton
15. agriculture
16. turkeys
17. Do grow
18. wandered
19. Did catch
20. balances
21. will arrive
22. chugged
23. imperative
24. interrogative
25. declarative

26. exclamatory

27. Can turkeys fly?

28. My uncle | found a diamond in Arkansas.

29. Laborers | are harvesting cotton and rice.

30. The Mississippi River | divides Arkansas and Mississippi.

LESSON 5   Complete Sentence or Sentence Fragment?

Practice 5

a. complete sentence

b. sentence fragment

c. sentence fragment

d. complete sentence

e. There

f. Their

g. homophones

More Practice 5   *(optional)*

1. sentence fragment
2. complete sentence
3. complete sentence
4. sentence fragment
5. sentence fragment
6. sentence fragment

Review Set 5

1. predicate
2. fragment
3. predicate
4. subject
5. predicate
6. homophones
7. there
8. pessimism

9. abundant

10. synonyms

11. complete sentence

12. sentence fragment

13. complete sentence

14. sentence fragment

15. sentence fragment

16. sentence fragment

17. complete sentence

18. complete sentence

19. California

20. forty-niners

21. you

22. Does have

23. came

24. Have climbed

25. exclamatory

26. declarative

27. imperative

28. interrogative

29. Who burned the toast?

30. California | has the tallest and oldest trees in the world.

LESSON 6   Correcting a Sentence Fragment

Practice 6

a. I found a big silver nugget.

b. An enormous dinosaur once lived here.

c. My best friend laughs at my jokes.

d. The tiger was sharpening its claws.

e. It's

f. its

More Practice 6

1. A mean-looking, bearded pirate guards the treasure.

2. A box of gold coins lies in a cave.

3. I would like to find the coins.

4. My friend and I searched the cave.

5. A bear makes its home in the cave.

Review Set 6

1. their

2. optimism

3. scarce

4. antonyms

5. Essential

6. it's

7. interrogative

8. predicate

9. action

10. exclamatory

11. sentence fragment

12. complete sentence

13. sentence fragment

14. complete sentence

15. We plan to hike Pike's Peak.

16. My favorite place in the whole world is Rocky Mountain National Park in Colorado.

17. Cattle are grazing in the meadow.

18. Two bald eagles landed on the mountain top.

19. snow

20. falcon

21. miners

22. fell

23. sits

24. Did find
25. declarative
26. interrogative
27. imperative
28. exclamatory
29. Ranchers irrigate their fields.
30. Bighorn sheep | dot Colorado's slopes.

LESSON 7 Action Verbs

Practice 7

a. influenced
b. spotted, admired
c. named
d. conceal
e. disclose

Review Set 7

1. disclose
2. its
3. their
4. Pessimism
5. abundant
6. visited
7. manufacture
8. included
9. clucked, scratched
10. breached, blew
11. sentence fragment
12. sentence fragment
13. complete sentence
14. complete sentence
15. A noisy helicopter landed on the beach.
16. I hope to see the Statue of Liberty.

17. A delicious snack food is an apple.
18. Dad was photographing Niagara Falls.
19. products
20. roses
21. lobster
22. contribute
23. Are blooming
24. is
25. exclamatory
26. interrogative
27. declarative
28. imperative
29. The lobster pinched me!
30. Lobster | flourishes off the coast of Connecticut.

LESSON 8 Capitalizing Proper Nouns

Practice 8

a. The Dutch formed a whaling colony in 1631.
b. They named the colony Lewes.
c. Let's read the book *Hans Brinker or the Silver Skates*.
d. The capital city of Delaware is Dover.
e. In 1609, Henry Hudson sailed into Delaware Bay.
f. geo-
g. geography
h. Geology

More Practice 8 *See Master Worksheets*

Review Set 8

1. earth
2. conceal

3. it's

4. their

5. scarce

6. Noxingtown Pond

7. Lynne Reid Banks, *The Indian in the Cupboard*

8. French, Delaware

9. tiptoes, makes

10. Have nibbled

11. sentence fragment

12. complete sentence

13. sentence fragment

14. complete sentence

15. Migrating ducks and geese are quacking and honking.

16. The peach blossoms smell heavenly.

17. Katy learned to play the trombone.

18. A blue hen from Delaware laid an egg.

19. cabins

20. salamander

21. geese

22. were built

23. swam

24. Are resting

25. imperative

26. declarative

27. interrogative

28. exclamatory

29. Do oranges grow in Delaware?

30. Delaware | was the first state in the union.

LESSON 9   Present Tense of Verbs

Practice 9

a. archipelago

b. estuary

c. washes

d. wishes

e. replies

f. tries

Review Set 9

1. river

2. geography

3. uncover

4. it's

5. Their

6. Friday, Kennedy Space Center

7. catches

8. flies

9. flock

10. opens, snaps

11. sentence fragment

12. sentence fragment

13. complete sentence

14. sentence fragment

15. A crocodile in the Everglades chased a turtle.

16. Laborers were picking bushels of juicy oranges.

17. Would you like to vacation in the Sunshine State?

18. An aggressive, grayish-brown mockingbird attacked a cat!

19. Juan Ponce de León

20. panthers

21. crocodile

22. claimed

23. Do live

24. crawled

25. imperative

26. exclamatory

27. interrogative

28. declarative

29. Drink plenty of water.

30. My friend from Michigan | enjoys Florida's warm winters.

LESSON 10 Past Tense of Regular Verbs

Practice 10

a. fauna

b. flora

c. clapped

d. buried

e. dropped

f. raced

g. dried

h. hiked

i. dipped

j. stepped

k. escaped

l. swallowed

Review Set 10

1. bird

2. archipelago

3. geology

4. hide

5. its

6. Florida's, Tallahassee, Maclay Gardens

7. hisses

8. fries

9. putt, chip, drive

10. squeezed, drank

11. sentence fragment

12. sentence fragment

13. complete sentence

14. complete sentence

15. Bumper-to-bumper traffic on the highway slowed our progress.

16. Someone is growing large, delicious peaches.

17. My dog Rover is the friendliest animal of all.

18. Would you like to become the President of the United States?

19. gin

20. otter

21. parade

22. Does separate

23. dove

24. comes

25. chatted

26. picked

27. a. clipped
    b. tried
    c. chatted
    d. denied

28. declarative

29. Jimmy Carter came from Georgia

30. Mills in Georgia | make paper from trees.

LESSON 11 Concrete, Abstract, and Collective Nouns

Practice 11

a. isthmus

b. peninsula

c. concrete

d. abstract

e. abstract

f. concrete

g. bushel

h. colony

More Practice 11

1. abstract

2. concrete

3. concrete

4. abstract

5. concrete

6. abstract

7. abstract

8. concrete

9. concrete

10. concrete

11. concrete

12. abstract

13. class, collection

14. school, fleet

15. swarm, assortment

Review Set 11

1. weed

2. estuary

3. earth

4. antonyms

5. it's

6. Gulf of Mexico, Hurricane Rita

7. kisses

8. flies

9. depicts

10. lived, worked

11. sentence fragment

12. complete sentence

13. sentence fragment

14. complete sentence

15. An aggressive alligator in the Okefenokee swamp opens its mouth.

16. We need to protect endangered animals.

17. a. concrete
    b. abstract
    c. concrete
    d. abstract

18. gaggle

19. Daniel Boone

20. stallion

21. Secretariat

22. led

23. Did race

24. goes

25. named

26. baked

27. a. chopped
    b. fried
    c. pitted
    d. replied

28. exclamatory

29. That cave is deep!

30. Georgia's nickname, the Empire State of the South,| refers to its size and wealth.

LESSON 12   Helping Verbs

Practice 12

a. is, am, are, was, were, be, being, been, has, have, had, may, might, must, can, could, do, does, did, shall, will, should, would.

b. (must)(have)(been) harvesting

c. (should)(have) called

d. (could)(have) helped

e. (shall) volunteer

f. strait

g. lagoon

More Practice 12 *See Master Worksheets*

Review Set 12

1. peninsula

2. flora

3. islands

4. geo-

5. disclose

6. tapped

7. turned

8. Rosalba, University, Hawaii, Manoa

9. tries

10. misses

11. paddled

12. exports, imports

13. is, am, are, was, were, be, being, been, has, have, had, may, might, must, can, could, do, does, did, shall, will, should, would

14. (will)(be) surfing

15. (should)(have) seen

16. sentence fragment

17. complete sentence

18. complete sentence

19. sentence fragment

20. My favorite summertime activities are swimming and reading.

21. a. concrete
    b. abstract
    c. abstract
    d. concrete

22. pod, team

23. volcano

24. goose

25. is

26. flew

27. a. jogged
    b. relied
    c. mopped
    d. dried

28. exclamatory

29. The Hawaiian alphabet has twelve letters.

30. My cousin on Maui | has planted a macadamia nut tree.

LESSON 13 — Singular, Plural, Compound, and Possessive Nouns

Practice 13

a. plural

b. singular

c. singular

d. plural

e. son-in-law, check mark, doorknob

f. Idaho's

g. collectors'

h. delta

i. tributary

More Practice 13 *See "Corny Chronicle #1" in Master Worksheets*

Review Set 13

1. water

2. water

3. fauna

4. estuary

5. Nonessential

6. rubbed

7. walked

8. plural

9. Shoshone, Sacagawea, Lewis, Clark, Bitterroot Range

10. hurries

11. brushes

12. leaps, digs, chases

13. is, am, are, was, were, be, being, been, has, have, had, may, might, must, can, could, do, does, did, shall, will, should, would

14. (was) built

15. (might) ride

16. complete sentence

17. sentence fragment

18. earth-dweller, trail blazer, pathfinder,

19. Idaho's

20. I would like to pick bing cherries near Boise, Idaho.

21. a. concrete
    b. abstract
    c. abstract
    d. concrete

22. crop

23. mountains

24. Ms. Garcia

25. are

26. Has been skiing

27. a. slipped
    b. hurried
    c. scrubbed
    d. replied

28. interrogative

29. Eat your green vegetables

30. A band of mountain men | have been telling tall tales.

LESSON 14   Future Tense

Practice 14

a. present

b. future

c. future

d. past

e. telephoned

f. will prove

g. talks

h. will

i. shall

j. will

k. shall

l. meridian

m. hemisphere

Review Set 14

1. tributary

2. lagoon

3. land

4. Fauna

5. Earth's

6. carried

7. shall

8. singular

9. Florida, Atlantic Ocean, Gulf of Mexico

10. worries

11. rushes

12. shuffles, dart

13. is, am, are, was, were, be, being, been, has, have, had, may, might, must, can, could, do, does, did, shall, will, should, would

14. (had) perfected

15. past tense

16. sentence fragment

17. complete sentence

18. place mat, cookbook

19. state's

20. We should be eating more fresh fruits and vegetables.

21. a. concrete
    b. abstract
    c. concrete
    d. abstract

22. crew

23. hero

24. shall pull

25. can buy

26. May borrow

27. a. dipped
    b. married
    c. rubbed
    d. buried

28. declarative

29. Shall we plow the field?

30. The Great Chicago Fire | destroyed much of the city in 1871.

LESSON 15 Capitalization: Sentence, Pronoun I, Poetry

Practice 15

a. In, March, I, Indianapolis, Indiana

b. Listen, Of, Paul Revere, On, April, Hardly, Who

c. The, Ohio River, Indiana

d. longitude

e. latitude

More Practice 15 *See Master Worksheets*

Review Set 15

1. meridian

2. stream

3. pond

4. isthmus

5. antonym

6. worked, their

7. shall, there

8. plural

9. The Isthmus of Panama connects North America with South America.

10. carries

11. polishes

12. sailed, crossed

13. where

14. (has) (been) playing

15. future tense

16. sentence fragment

17. complete sentence

18. playground, footprint

19. Longfellow's, Paul Revere's

20. I would love to ride a galloping horse.

21. a. abstract
    b. concrete
    c. concrete
    d. abstract

22. drove

23. residents

24. shall bake

25. work

26. Birds of a feather flock together,
    And so will pigs and swine;
    Rats and mice will have their choice,
    And so will I have mine.

27. a. hugged
    b. skipped
    c. hopped
    d. bullied

28. imperative

29. Abe Lincoln's log cabin is in Indiana.

30. John Chapman | planted apple trees from Pennsylvania to Illinois.

LESSON 16 Irregular Plural Nouns, Part 1

Practice 16

a. atoll

b. arroyo

c. mosses

d. lakes

e. donkeys

f. brushes

g. Burgesses

h. boundaries

i. deltas

j. wrenches

k. days

l. taxes

m. turkeys

n. toys

o. berries

p. puppies

Review Set 16

1. latitude

2. meridian

3. triangle

4. lagoon

5. Optimism

6. trimmed, their

7. shall, there

8. never

9. Yes, I think Julia lives near the Mississippi River, in Memphis, Tennessee.

10. fries

11. waxes

12. believes, expects

13. munch

14. (was) born

15. future tense

16. complete sentence

17. sentence fragment

18. toothbrush, mailbox

19. Daniel Boone's

20. Example: A strong, thoroughbred race horse speeds around the track.

21. a. abstract
    b. abstract
    c. concrete
    d. concrete

22. cast

23. daughter

24. shall answer

25. Did survive

26. Mary had a little lamb.
    Its fleece was white as snow.
    And everywhere that Mary went
    The lamb was sure to go.

27. tried

28. interrogative

29. a. keys
    b. babies

c. lunches

d. cherries

30. Colorful American goldfinches | peck at thistle seeds.

LESSON 17   Irregular Plural Nouns, part 2

Practice 17

a. cliffs

b. tomatoes

c. chiefs

d. knives

e. salmon

f. teeth

g. geese

h. cellos

i. zoos

l. Tropic of Capricorn

m. Tropic of Cancer

More Practice 17

1. crosses

2. bunches

3. boys

4. lunches

5. bushes

6. bosses

7. cherries

8. bays

9. sheep

10. men

11. ladies

12. women

13. people

14. mice

15. geese

16. cliffs

17. leaves

18. loaves

19. altos

20. potatoes

Review Set 17

1. lagoon

2. longitude

3. hemispheres

4. delta

5. its

6. sipped, their

7. It's

8. plural

9. Every Sunday, Juan jogs down Myrtle Street in Monrovia, California.

10. replies

11. wishes

12. believes, expects

13. dip

14. (Have) tasted

15. past tense

16. complete sentence

17. sentence fragment

18. railroad, spaceship

19. pelican's

20. A brown pelican with its long gray bill caught a dozen fish.

21. a. abstract
    b. concrete
    c. abstract
    d. concrete

22. colony

23. Mardi Gras

24. shall paint

25. May taste

26. Twinkle, twinkle, little star.
    How I wonder what you are,
    Up above the world so high,
    Like a diamond in the sky.

27. clapped

28. declarative

29. a. pianos
    b. benches
    c. lives
    d. children

30. The people of Louisiana | listen to Cajun
    music.

LESSON 18 Irregular Verbs, Part 1: Be, Have, Do

Practice 18

a. are

b. has

c. does

d. had

e. were

f. did

g. timberline

h. Torrid Zone

More Practice 18

1. a. am
   b. are
   c. is
   d. are

2. a. have
   b. have
   c. has
   d. have

3. a. do
   b. do
   c. does
   d. do

4. a. was
   b. were
   c. was
   d. were

5. does

6. has

7. was

8. Are

9. were

10. are

11. Were

12. Was

13. has

14. Does

15. am

16. did

Review Set 18

1. equator

2. coral reef

3. Longitude

4. hemispheres

5. isthmus

6. were, called

7. It's, there

8. are, their

9. This February, I would like to sail to
   Catalina Island.

10. dries

11. washes

12. feeds, visits

13. bill

14. (might) (have) painted

15. present tense

16. complete sentence

17. sentence fragment

18. baseball, earthworm

19. Maine's

20. An active little chickadee with a black cap calls to the other chickadees.

21. a. abstract
    b. concrete
    c. abstract
    d. concrete

22. herd

23. Leif Erickson

24. were

25. Was built

26. A diller, a dollar, a ten o'clock scholar!
    What makes you come so soon?
    You used to come at ten o'clock;
    Now you come at noon.

27. dropped

28. exclamatory

29. a. sheep
    b. churches
    c. thieves
    d. potatoes

30. Maine | has a jagged coastline with rocky cliffs.

LESSON 19   Four Principal Parts of Verbs

Practice 19

a. (is) acting, acted, (has) acted

b. (is) wanting, wanted, (has) wanted

c. (is) walking, walked, (has) walked

d. (is) viewing, viewed, (has) viewed

e. (is) working, worked, (has) worked

f. tundra

g. savanna

Review Set 19

1. timberline

2. tropic

3. atoll

4. Latitude

5. water

6. does

7. It's, there

8. has

9. present

10. Is Salem, Oregon, in the Willamette Valley?

11. applies

12. mows, sweeps

13. far

14. (Does) have

15. present tense

16. sentence fragment

17. complete sentence

18. sunflower, moonlight

19. country's

20. My ancestors were brave to sail across the Atlantic Ocean.

21. a. concrete
    b. abstract
    c. abstract
    d. concrete

22. family

23. Clarissa

24. has

25. Has been jousting

26. I scream,
You scream,
We all scream
For ice cream!

27. a. (is) mixing
b. mixed
c. (has) mixed

28. declarative

29. a. berries
b. monkeys
c. halves
d. tomatoes

30. A long bridge | stretches across the Chesapeake Bay.

LESSON 20   Simple Prepositions, Part 1

Practice 20

a. aboard, about, above, across, after, against, along, alongside, amid, among, around, at, before, behind, below, beneath

b. beside, besides, between, beyond, but, by, concerning, considering, despite, down, during, except, excepting, for, from, in

c. *See preposition list*

d. At, for

e. from, to

f. near, off, of

g. chasm

h. mesas

More Practice 20

1. above, after, around, before, below

2. between, but, down, excepting, from

3. for, over, through

4. along, at

5. to, around

6. Opposite

7. During, with

8. without, on

Review Set 20

1. tropical

2. Trees

3. Capricorn

4. atoll

5. disclose

6. am

7. its, there

8. does

9. past

10. At the store, I bought Washington apples, Idaho potatoes, and Wisconsin cheese.

11. mixes

12. gathers, milks, drives

13. mad

14. (has) (been) harvesting

15. past tense

16. sentence fragment

17. of, into

18. across, after, alongside, among, below

19. eyewitness's

20. I will be wearing a warm, woolen sweater on a cold, winter morning.

21. a. concrete
b. abstract
c. concrete
d. abstract

22. shipment

23. Kelloggs

24. had

25. Did make

26. On top of spaghetti
All covered with cheese,

I lost my poor meatball
When somebody sneezed.

27. a. (is) answering
    b. answered
    c. (has) answered

28. declarative

29. a. foxes
    b. discoveries
    c. butterflies
    d. ostriches

30. Both tart and sweet cherries | grow in Michigan.

LESSON 21 Simple Prepositions, Part 2

Practice 21

a. inside, into, like, near, of, off, on, onto, opposite, out, outside, over, past, regarding, round, save

b. since, through, throughout, till, to, toward, under, underneath, until, unto, up, upon, with, within, without

c. *See preposition lists*

d. During, of

e. Underneath, with

f. Since, in, from

g. fissure

h. plateau

More Practice 21

1. near, off, out, past, round

2. throughout, to, underneath, unto, with

3. V

4. N

5. P

6, V

7. P

8. N

9. V

10. P

11. N

12. P

13. V

14. N

15. P

16. V

17. P

18. P

19. N

20. P

21. N

22. V

Review Set 21

1. table

2. plain

3. timberline

4. Cancer

5. homophones

6. has

7. It's, there

8. does

9. past

10. In July, I shall visit the Smithsonian Institution in Washington, D.C.

11. copies

12. repairs, fills, sings

13. rust

14. (can) cultivate

15. present tense

16. sentence fragment

17. On, with, up, down

18. into, off, out, outside, round

19. factbook's

20. A Mississippi steamboat with two smoke stacks and a paddle wheel cruises up the river.

21. a. concrete
    b. abstract
    c. abstract
    d. concrete

22. flock

23. Jefferson Davis

24. were

25. Did grow

26. If all the world were paper,
    And all the sea were ink,
    If all the trees
    Were bread and cheese,
    What should we have to drink?

27. a. (is) laughing
    b. laughed
    c. (has) laughed

28. exclamatory

29. a. inches
    b. photocopies
    c. bluejays
    d. wolves

30. Grover and Annie Mae | raise catfish in their pond.

LESSON 22   Irregular Plural Nouns, Part 3

Practice 22

a. mothers-in-law

b. chiefs of staff

c. mouthfuls

d. pailfuls

e. placid

f. placare

g. placate

h. implacable

Review Set 22

1. crack

2. crack

3. tundra

4. equator

5. conceal

6. are

7. their, its

8. does

9. present

10. In our solar system, Mercury and Venus are the only planets without moons.

11. cashes

12. water, feed, left

13. wood

14. (may) follow

15. past tense

16. complete sentence

17. About, of, from

18. asked

19. storybook's

20. People are tapping their feet to country music.

21. a. concrete
    b. abstract
    c. abstract
    d. concrete

22. pack

23. fiddler

24. has

25. came

26. Red sky at night,
    Sailor's delight;
    Red sky at morning,
    Sailor's warning.

27. a. (is) sailing
    b. sailed
    c. (has) sailed

28. declarative

29. a. calves
    b. attorneys at law
    c. spoonfuls
    d. sheep

30. A white-haired fiddler in a plaid shirt |
    fiddled faster and faster.

LESSON 23 — Complete Sentence or Run-on Sentence?

Practice 23

a. run-on sentence

b. complete sentence

c. complete sentence

d. run-on sentence

e. talk

f. elocution

g. ventriloquist

More Practice 23

1. run-on sentence

2. complete sentence

3. run-on sentence

4. complete sentence (subject, *you*, understood)

5. run-on sentence

6. complete sentence (subject, *you*, understood)

Review Set 23

1. calmed

2. chasm

3. chasm

4. cold

5. earth's

6. were

7. it's, there

8. Does

9. past

10. One of Montana's richest gold deposits is in Virginia City.

11. mashes

12. made, signed, mailed

13. (have)(been) thriving

14. (Can) survive

15. future tense

16. Sentence fragment (missing predicate)

17. In, with

18. buy

19. gentleman's

20. Example: Someday I would like to canoe down the river through Montana's wild lands.

21. a. concrete
    b. concrete
    c. abstract
    d. abstract

22. herd

23. climbers

24. does

25. Have reached

26. I've been working on the railroad
    All the livelong day,
    I've been working on the railroad
    Just to pass the time away

27. a. (is) disclosing
    b. disclosed
    c. (has) disclosed

28. interrogative

29. a. shelves
    b. justices of the peace
    c. cupfuls
    d. deer

30. Two huge bison with thick brown coats |
    were minding their own business.

LESSON 24   Correcting a Run-on Sentence

Practice 24

a. My friends in Nebraska grow corn, and
   they also raise pigs.

b. Some ranchers felt lonely, so they had
   cornhusking parties with neighbors.

c. Corn grows well in Nebraska. Some of it
   is fed to livestock.

d. On the prairie, wood was scarce, so people
   built homes of sod.

e. strength

f. valor

g. valiant

More Practice 24

1. It's too dark. I can't see.

2. I have a map. Let's find the cave.

3. Please come with me. I need your help.

4. Bats live here. They sleep during the day.

5. Bats wake. They startle me!

Review Set 24

1. speaking

2. Implacable

3. fissure

4. mesa

5. arroyo

6. are

7. their, its

8. Have

9. present

10. Nebraska's capital, Lincoln, is named after
    President Abraham Lincoln.

11. magnifies

12. struts, pecks, calls

13. (Shall) follow

14. (have) (been) roping

15. present tense

16. run-on sentence

17. In, of, with

18. lake

19. Mr. Blue's

20. This is Arbor Day. We shall plant trees.

21. a. abstract
    b. abstract
    c. concrete
    d. concrete

22. committee

23. mammoths

24. shall be

25. were

26. O beautiful for spacious skies,
    For amber waves of grain,
    For purple mountain majesties
    Above the fruited plain!

27. a. (is) concealing
    b. concealed
    c. (has) concealed

28. imperative

29. a. estuaries
    b. sisters-in-law

c. fistfuls
d. countries

30. Cattle, corn, pigs, and oil | provide economic stability for Nebraska.

LESSON 25   Capitalization: Titles

Practice 25

a. *Winnie the Pooh*

b. *The Call of the Wild*

c. *The House at Pooh Corner*

d. "Home on the Range"

e. igneous rocks

f. ignis

g. ignite

More Practice 25   *See Master Worksheets*

Review Set 25

1. valiant
2. ventriloquist
3. calm
4. flat
5. Tundra
6. predicate
7. There, its
8. does
9. past
10. One of the world's biggest dams is Hoover Dam in Nevada.
11. flies
12. fell, tumbled, rolled
13. (Has) broken
14. *The Cat in the Hat*

15. future tense
16. complete sentence
17. In, around, under
18. tool
19. Nevada's
20. Prospectors went to Virginia City. There they found silver and gold.
21. a. concrete
    b. concrete
    c. abstract
    d. abstract
22. team
23. you
24. were
25. Have visited
26. People keep saying it's not good
    To learn things by heart,
    But pretty things well said—
    It's nice to have them in your head.
27. a. (is) igniting
    b. ignited
    c. (has) ignited
28. exclamatory
29. a. skies
    b. lords of England
    c. tubfuls
    d. prefixes
30. The state of Nevada | mines silver, copper, and turquoise.

LESSON 26   Capitalization: Outlines and Quotations

Practice 26

a. I. Types of trees
    A. Deciduous trees
    B. Evergreen trees

b. Andrew Angles said, "Your grandmother and I came from Scotland."

c. Then he explained, "It was difficult leaving our families."

d. metamorphosis

e. metamorphic rocks

f. metamorphosis

More Practice 26 *See Master Worksheets*

Review Set 26

1. rocks
2. brave
3. Elocution
4. peaceful
5. warm
6. abstract
7. it's, their
8. has
9. present
10. Joseph said, "The honeybee is New Jersey's state bug."
11. hisses
12. drives
13. ⟨should⟩ ⟨have⟩ offered
14. "I've Been Working on the Railroad"
15. past tense
16. sentence fragment
17. During, alongside, without
18. understand
19. Alabama's
20. New Jersey has beautiful beaches. People like to come to the shore.
21. I don't want to swim in the ocean with jellyfish, sharks, and eels.
22. lighthouse, landmark
23. New Jersey
24. are
25. lies
26. I. The globe
    A. Continents
    B. Oceans
    II. Locating places
    A. Hemispheres
    B. Latitude and longitude
27. a. (is) playing
    b. played
    c. (has) played
28. interrogative
29. a. ladies
    b. brothers-in-law
    c. shovelfuls
    d. men
30. The state of New Jersey | protects plants and animals in the Pine Barrens.

LESSON 27 Dictionary Information about a Word, Part 1

Practice 27

a. 1. a fight between forces
   2. to struggle or fight

b. noun

c. brothers, brethren

d. per·pen·dic·u·lar

e. dis klōz´

f. Sediment

g. Sedimentary rocks

Review Set 27

1. Metamorphic
2. molten
3. Valor
4. talks
5. Placid
6. concrete
7. its, there

8. does

9. past

10. Besly said, "Next Tuesday I shall take the train to Santa Fe, New Mexico."

11. fizzes

12. yawns, rubs

13. (might) (have) built

14. "The Hunting of the Great Bear"

15. future tense

16. run-on sentence

17. In, with, at

18. a. noun
    b. at´ ol

19. roadrunners'

20. Ilbea ate a chili pepper. Tears came to her eyes.

21. An unidentified flying object in the night sky disappeared quickly.

22. grove

23. roadrunner

24. has

25. runs

26. I. Products of New Mexico
    A. Agricultural products
    B. Industrial products

27. a. (is) crying
    b. cried
    c. (has) cried

28. declarative

29. a. echoes
    b. editors in chief
    c. knives
    d. cities

31. Migrants from the East | headed west by wagon train.

LESSON 28   Spelling Rules: Silent Letters k, g, w, t, d, and c

Practice 28

a. (w)res(t)le

b. (w)hose

c. (g)nome

d. lis(t)en

e. (k)not

f. (k)nees

g. s(c)enery

h. whis(t)le

i. magma

j. caldera

Review Set 28

1. layers

2. changed

3. burn

4. courage

5. essential

6. plural

7. It's, their

8. were

9. present

10. Rosa said, "My family and I saw two plays in New York City."

11. fishes

12. thinks, speaks

13. (must) (have) entered

14. "Ali Baba and the Forty Thieves"

15. past tense

16. sentence fragment

17. Despite, along, over, around, into

18. a. transitive verb
    b. ig zôlt´

19. a. (k)nead
    b. si(g)n
    c. wa(t)ch

20. The Niagara River has magnificent waterfalls. Have you seen them?

21. Someday I shall take the elevator to the eighty-sixth floor of the Empire State Building.

22. gateway

23. glaciers

24. were

25. Did create

26. An apple a day
    Keeps the doctor away.

27. a. (is) drying
    b. dried
    c. (has) dried

28. exclamatory

29. a. logos
    b. bookshelves
    c. pailfuls
    d. counties

30. The Erie Canal | links the Atlantic and the Great Lakes.

LESSON 29   Spelling Rules: Silent Letters p, b, l, u, h, n, and gh

Practice 29

a. g(u)ess

b. althou(gh)

c. (c)horus

d. (r)hyme

e. cou(l)d

f. ca(l)f

g. si(gh)t

h. cor(p)s

i. (p)neumonia

j. de(b)t

k. tom(b)

l. yo(l)k

m. meteor

n. meteorite

Review Set 29

1. rock

2. rocks

3. metamorphosis

4. ignite

5. synonym

6. concrete

7. There, its

8. did

9. past

10. The ship's captain said, "While out at sea, I spotted Cape Hatteras Lighthouse, warning me of hazardous waters ahead."

11. applies

12. warns, lights

13. (might) (have) crashed

14. "The Arrow and the Song"

15. future tense

16. complete sentence

17. After, through, around, into, for

18. a. adjective
    b. plas´ id

19. a. (know)
    b. light
    c. lim(b)

20. Orville and Wilbur Wright successfully flew for the first time in 1903. They departed from Kitty Hawk, North Carolina.

21. The notorious pirate Blackbeard terrorized the high seas.

22. shipment

23. furniture

24. has

25. Was crafted

26. I. Florida's wetlands
    A. The world's largest swamp
    B. Endangered species

27. a. (is) doing
    b. did
    c. (has) done

28. imperative

29. a. trout
    b. children of the King
    c. axes
    d. industries

30. Many ships | have sunk off the coast of North Carolina.

LESSON 30 Dictionary Information about a Word, Part 2

Practice 30

a. Latin

b. Anatomy

c. permit or allow

d. vertebrate

e. invertebrate

Review Set 30

1. meteorite

2. magma

3. Sediment

4. change

5. scarce

6. possessive

7. etymology

8. similar

9. skipped

10. Lilah asked, "Have you ever experienced a North Dakota blizzard?"

11. qualifies

12. stings, bites, whistles

13. (can) teach

14. *Why the Chicken Crossed the Road*

15. past tense

16. run-on sentence

17. At, on, through, for, of, with, in

18. a. noun
    b. pla tō´
    c. French

19. a. bri(d)ge
    b. (h)our
    c. ta(l)k

20. Little ground squirrels flick their tails. Then they dive back into their burrows on the prairie.

21. I dream of growing sunflowers over ten feet tall.

22. waterfowl

23. insects

24. shall harvest

25. came

26. a. (is) trying
    b. tried
    c. (has) tried

27. interrogative

28. The cock doth crow
    To let you know,
    If you be wise,
    Tis time to rise.

29. a. wives
    b. spoonfuls
    c. keys
    d. countries

30. All the giant golden sunflowers | turn their
    faces to the sunshine.

LESSON 31   Linking Verbs

Practice 31

a. is, am are, was, were, be, being, been,
    look, feel, taste, smell, sound, seem,
    appear, grow, become, remain, stay

b. *See list above*

c. became

d. was

e. appears

f. remains

g. seems

h. sounds

i. no linking verb

j. smells

k. liability

l. asset

More Practice 31

1. seems
2. remains
3. stayed
4. felt
5. appeared
6. tastes
7. grew

8. smells
9. become
10. sounded
11. action
12. linking
13. action
14. linking
15. action
16. linking

Review Set 31

1. invertebrate
2. meteor
3. Magma
4. liquid
5. pessimism
6. abstract
7. verb
8. opposite
9. hopped
10. Mr. Chen said, "The famous ballerina
    Maria Tallchief was a Native American
    from Fairfax, Oklahoma.
11. cashes
12. counted, considered
13. (might) (have) counted
14. "America the Beautiful"
15. grew
16. complete sentence
17. of, during, to
18. a. adjective
    b. liv´ id
    c. French (from Latin)

19. a. whose
    b. sigh
    c. folk

20. Pam lives in Oklahoma City. Her husband works in the oil fields.

21. Example: We ran to escape the tornado.

22. spray

23. Sooners

24. fries

25. claimed

26. a. (is) worrying
    b. worried
    c. (has) worried

27. exclamatory

28. I. Resources of Oklahoma
    A. Oil
    B. Cattle
    C. Wheat

29. a. sheep
    b. sisters-in-law
    c. donkeys
    d. liabilities

30. Oklahoma's twisters | must have surprised the settlers.

LESSON 32 Diagramming Simple Subjects and Simple Predicates

Practice 32

a. trees | cover

b. hazelnuts | taste

c. owls | hoot

d. you | Do fish

e. Pan American

f. Pan

g. panacea

Review Set 32

1. antonyms

2. invertebrate

3. meteor

4. depression

5. There

6. plural

7. left

8. right

9. mopped

10. Jamaica King said, "The people of Oregon care about their environment."

11. mashes

12. blast, create

13. (have) (been) banned

14. "Chased by the Trail"

15. feels

16. sentence fragment

17. Since, within, of

18. a. adjective
    b. sə rēn´
    c. Latin

19. a. who
    b. high
    c. guard

20. Oregon's Columbia River has a strong current. It powers plants that provide electricity.

21. is, am, are, was, were, be, being, been, look, feel, taste, smell, sound, seem, appear, grow, become, remain, stay

22. lighthouse

23. fried

24. a. (is) carrying
    b. carried
    c. (has) carried

25. imperative

26. Sweet Katrina's neat pet beaver
    Came to stay and wouldn't leave her.

27. a. boxes
    b. mugfuls
    c. Tuesdays
    d. abilities

28. <u>pirates</u> | <u>go</u>

29. <u>hoodlum</u> | <u>looks</u>

30. <u>pirate</u> | <u>Has boarded</u>

LESSON 33   Spelling Rules: Suffixes, Part 1

Practice 33

a. beautiful

b. gloominess

c. merriest

d. cheerily

e. plateful

f. biting

g. lively

h. driver

i. knowledgeable

j. rating

k. clueless

l. indispensable

m. dispensable

Review Set 33

1. pan

2. disadvantage

3. backbone

4. sky

5. It's

6. abstract

7. a. reliable
   b. playing

8. a. loving
   b. careful

9. denied

10. Miss Fortune said, "I lost my purse in Pennsylvania."

11. brushes

12. sits, binds

13. (must) (have) misplaced

14. "The Merchant of Venice"

15. remains

16. run-on sentence

17. Without, of

18. a. noun
    b. bō kā′
    c. French

19. a. walk
    b. design
    c. (knot)

20. On February 2, Punxsutawney Phil saw his shadow. He predicts six more weeks of winter.

21. is, am, are, was, were, be, being, been, look, feel, taste, smell, sound, seem, appear, grow, become, remain, stay

22. colony

23. grinned

24. a. (is) marrying
    b. married
    c. (has) married

25. interrogative

26. I. Pennsylvania's agriculture
    A. Dairy products
    B. Fresh vegetables
    C. Eggs

27. a. faxes
    b. men
    c. piccolos
    d. duties

28. friends | come

29. player | seems

30. team | Did win

LESSON 34   Spelling Rules: Suffixes, Part 2

Practice 34

a. tapped

b. stopping

c. gladly

d. benefited

e. flatness

f. proclamation

g. clamor

h. Clamare

Review Set 34

1. synonyms

2. Pan

3. liability

4. backbone

5. archipelago

6. possessive

7. a. glorious
   b. scary

8. a. winning
   b. gladly

9. clapped

10. "No," said Miss Fortune, "I did not leave my purse at a bus station in Philadelphia."

11. rushes

12. left, started

13. (has)(been) fishing

14. *Gone with the Wind*

15. looks

16. sentence fragment

17. near, of

18. a. noun
    b. en´ klāv
    c. French (from Latin)

19. a. (wrote
    b. edge
    c. hym(n)

20. Example: The state of Rhode Island is the smallest in area.

21. is, am, are, was, were, be, being, been, look, feel, taste, smell, sound, seem, appear, grow, become, remain, stay

22. Tugboats

23. grins

24. a. (is) hurrying
    b. hurried
    c. (has) hurried

25. declarative

26. A wise old owl sat in an oak;
    The more he heard, the less he spoke;
    The less he spoke, the more he heard;
    Why aren't we all like that wise old bird?

27. a. taxes
    b. women
    c. letters of reference
    d. duties

28. cow | leaps

29. <u>cow</u> | <u>appears</u>

30. <u>cow</u> | <u>Will return</u>

LESSON 35

Spelling Rules: ie or ei

Practice 35

a. achieve

b. piece

c. receive

d. conceit

e. freight

f. feign

g. kin

h. Akin

Review Set 35

1. proclamation

2. indispensable

3. all

4. asset

5. Flora

6. concrete

7. a. flier
   b. coming

8. a. shopped
   b. warmest

9. a. believe
   b. receive

10. Miss Fortune asked, "Have you seen my purse?"

11. expresses

12. clucked, laid

13. (have)(been) weaving

14. "King Arthur and the Round Table"

15. proved

16. complete sentence

17. After, through

18. a. verb
    b. dik´ tāt
    c. Latin

19. a. com(b)
    b. glis(t)en
    c. (p)salm

20. Example: South Carolina is the Palmetto State. Its capital is Columbia.

21. far

22. flock

23. will smile

24. a. (is) moving
    b. moved
    c. (has) moved

25. declarative

26. Use *i* before *e*
    Except after *c*
    Or when sounded like *ay*
    As in *neighbor* and *weigh*

27. a. inches
    b. deer
    c. sons-in-law
    d. dairies

28. <u>cow</u> | <u>comes</u>

29. <u>laugh</u> | <u>sounds</u>

30. <u>dish</u> | <u>Does run</u>

LESSON 36

Phrases and Clauses

Practice 36

a. clause

b. phrase

c. clause

d. phrase

e. concert | began

f. they | sang

g. David Crockett | remains

h. avaricious

i. avarice

Review Set 36

1. family

2. announcement

3. Dispensable

4. all

5. There

6. plural

7. a. readily
   b. player

8. a. biggest
   b. wishful

9. a. chief
   b. ceiling

10. The docent at Graceland said, "Here is Mr. Presley's study."

11. presses

12. clause

13. (might) (have) impressed

14. "The Hawaiian Wedding Song"

15. became

16. run-on sentence

17. around, under, through

18. a. noun
    b. di´ graf
    c. Greek

19. a. (knee)
    b. s(c)ent
    c. (honor)

20. Some people like to explore deep, dark caves.

21. pound

22. sunglasses

23. shall smile

24. a. (is) studying
    b. studied
    c. (has) studied

25. interrogative

26. I. Animal husbandry in Tennessee
    A. Poultry
    B. Pigs
    C. Horses

27. a. ranches
    b. cattle
    c. church mice
    d. diaries

28. Van | will sing   you | will play

29. dish | runs

30. (you) | catch

LESSON 37   Diagramming a Direct Object

Practice 37

a. chili

b. (none)

c. lasso

d. Texans | eat | chili

e. rancher | is twirling | lasso

f. encumbrance

g. encumber

Review Set 37

1. Avarice
2. akin
3. clamare
4. unessential
5. peninsula
6. abstract
7. a. modifier
   b. sensible
8. a. funny
   b. madness
9. a. brief
   b. deceive
10. A newscaster reported, "Oil production increased in Texas this year."
11. munches
12. phrase
13. (could) (have) lassoed
14. "The Children's Hour"
15. grew
16. complete sentence
17. on, with
18. a. noun
    b. kup´ lit
    c. French
19. a. ba(d)ge
    b. recei(p)t
    c. thou(gh)t
20. Example: The frog leaped from the water. It landed on my shoe.
21. disappear
22. herd
23. ripped

24. a. (is) ripping
    b. ripped
    c. (has) ripped
25. exclamatory
26. Grammar rules are fun to learn, But an *A* is hard to earn.
27. a. roaches
    b. solos
    c. teaspoonfuls
    d. libraries
28. Van | has been singing

    Jan | has been playing
29. Robert | is reading | novel
30. Christie | Has found | accordian

LESSON 38   Capitalization: People Titles, Family Words, School Subjects

Practice 38

a. Are, Spanish

b. I, Grandpa

c. Have, Dr. U. B. Straight

d. I

e. exalt

f. humiliate

More Practice 38   *See Master Worksheets*

Review Set 38

1. encumber
2. synonyms
3. Akin
4. clamor
5. strait
6. possessive

7. a. sunnier
   b. admiration

8. a. beginning
   b. sadness

9. a. shield
   b. perceive

10. Ms. Lim asked, "Have you tried the Texas cheese bread?"

11. pacifies

12. clause

13. (should)(have) seen

14. Yes, Mom is taking a Spanish class from Professor Lopez.

15. looks

16. sentence fragment

17. along, of

18. a. adjective
    b. d ī dak´ tik
    c. Greek

19. a. com(b)
    b. ha(l)f
    c. rei(g)n

20. Example: People were fishing for marlin near Padre Island.

21. where

22. raincoat

23. snipped

24. a. (is) snipping
    b. snipped
    c. (has) snipped

25. imperative

26. I. Produce from Texas
    A. Bunches of carrots
    B. Bags of peanuts

27. a. anniversaries
    b. birthdays
    c. queens of England

28. Pac | was trimming

    Jud | was examining

29. Tyler | Has polished | shoes

30. Florinda | might have left | trumpet

LESSON 39   Descriptive Adjectives

Practice 39

a. old, rusty

b. Healthful, delicious

c. ripe, juicy

d. lively, friendly (*answers will vary*)

e. deep, loud (*answers will vary*)

f. warm, fuzzy (*answers will vary*)

g. dogma

h. dogmatic

More Practice 39   *See Corny Chronicle #2 in Master Worksheets.*

Review Set 39

1. shame

2. burden

3. avaricious

4. similar

5. It's

6. abstract

7. a. pitiful
   b. said

8. a. dropping
   b. warmer

9. a. view
   b. neighbor

10. enormous, salty

11. reaches

12. phrase

13. (Has) (been) floating

14. *The Swiss Family Robinson*

15. remains

16. run-on sentence

17. On, down, until

18. a. adjective
    b. dij´ i tāt
    c. Latin

19. a. (k)neel
    b. t(w)o
    c. g(u)ard

20. Example: In Utah's Great Salt Lake, floating is easy, but swimming under water is difficult.

21. paste

22. cluster

23. shall sing

24. a. (is) snapping
    b. snapped
    c. (has) snapped

25. heavy, holey, black, stylish, new, large, small, old, curious, empty, etc.

26. I have a hunch
    It's time for lunch.

27. a. dictionaries
    b. avocados
    c. rulers of Spain

28. teacher | asks   Perlina | scratches

29. Perlina | has been counting | freckles

30. Perlina | is rubbing | eyes

LESSON 40 — The Limiting Adjective • Diagramming Adjectives

Practice 40

a. tangible

b. intangible

c. Juan's, several

d. Some, the

e. This, two

f. That, my

g. Amir | plays | bells \ these \ golden

More Practice 40 *See Master Worksheets*

Review Set 40

1. dogmatic

2. embarrass

3. encumber

4. greed

5. placare

6. plural

7. a. craziness
   b. paid

8. a. mopped
   b. raining

9. a. priest
   b. receipt

10. Lush, colorful, appreciative

11. relies

12. clause

13. (Should) (have) stuck

14. Sergeant Smug asked Mom if she passed her fourth grade English class.

15. seems

16. complete sentence

17. underneath, near

18. a. noun
    b. ra pôr′
    c. French (going back to Latin)

19. a. sign
    b. listen
    c. honesty

20. Example: Luey is pouring maple syrup on the pancakes.

21. blow

22. This, Max's, two, several, his

23. emptied

24. a. (is) emptying
    b. emptied
    c. (has) emptied

25. weary, young, happy, old, frantic, energetic, sleepy, serious, suspicious, sneaky, etc.

26. "There is a copy of *The Wizard of Oz* on Ms. Blue's bookshelf."

27. a. Mondays
    b. brushes
    c. private investigators

28. others | are taking   Perlina | is chewing

29. Mr. Hake | can wiggle | ears
    his

30. you | Can wiggle | ears
    your

LESSON 41   Capitalization: Areas, Religions, Greetings

Practice 41

a. These passages are from the King James Bible.

b. When I…East, I….

c. Look

d. Dear Dad,
   I am having fun at camp.
       Your son,
       Alex

e. cognizant

f. cognizance

Review Set 41

1. intangible

2. authoritative

3. praise

4. encumbrance

5. Mesa

6. possessive

7. a. laziness
   b. daily

8. a. committed
   b. cloudless

9. a. niece
   b. deceit

10. Fertile, tasty

11. Nancy attends a Lutheran church in the Northeast.

12. phrase

13. (Has) (been) hiking

14. "A Bicycle Built for Two"

15. appears

16. sentence fragment

17. in, near, beneath

18. a. noun
    b. durth
    c. Middle English

19. a. design
    b. lamb
    c. hourly

20. Crossing the Connecticut River is a covered bridge. It is one of the longest in the world.

21. declarative

22. Max's, many, his, two, that

23. empties

24. a. (is) spying
    b. spied
    c. (has) spied

25. red, messy, black, curly, long, shiny, short, blonde, straight, gray

26. Mortimer asked, "How many copies of *Robinson Crusoe* does Mr. Lopez have?

27. a. copies
    b. axes
    c. secret agents

28. Perlina | was solving

    classmates | were sleeping

29. Perlina | is taking | test
    a / difficult

30. Perlina | Will pass | test
    this

LESSON 42 Proper Adjectives

Practice 42

a. Italian sausage

b. Renaissance fair

c. Scottish bagpipes

d. Chinese martial arts

e. Bob | wore | shirt
   a / Hawaiian

f. Frugal

g. Extravagant

Review Set 42

1. antonyms

2. Tangible

3. Dogma

4. exalt

5. *loqui*

6. concrete

7. a. readily
   b. coming

8. a. winning
   b. rained

9. a. relieve
   b. freight

10. French, Canadian

11. Dear Quan,
    Please don't eat all of the Canadian bacon.
    Your brother,
    Sheung

12. clause

13. (might) (have) heard

14. Next semester, Dad will take Mr. Castro's Spanish class.

15. sound

16. run-on sentence

17. throughout, about, beyond

18. a. noun
    b. dis´ taf
    c. Old English

19. a. (k)not
    b. (w)ritten
    c. clim(b)

20. Example: Would you like to taste cheese from Wisconsin?

21. flea

22. her, three, the, Martinez's, that

23. shall feed

24. a. (is) wrapping
    b. wrapped
    c. has wrapped

25. sweaty, tired, energetic, happy, tall, skinny, short, muscular, friendly, elderly

26. It's raining, it's pouring,
    The old man is snoring…

27. a. branches
    b. calves
    d. sons-in-law

28. bell | rang   Ms. Hoo | stood

    class | applauded

29. brother | has saved | shoelaces
    (My frugal) (his old)

30. you | Have saved | shoelaces
    (your old)

LESSON 43   No Capital Letter

Practice 43

a. maternal

b. paternal

c. no additional capital letter

d. no additional capital letter

e. Chinese

f. We

g. Twenty-four

More Practice 43   *See Master Worksheets*

Review Set 43

1. Frugal

2. Cognizance

3. touch

4. belief

5. talk

6. collective

7. a. steadily
   b. peaceful

8. a. sipping
   b. broadest

9. a. weigh
   b. achieve

10. Russian, Australian

11. My Jewish friend Lenny won the chess championship in the Western division.

12. phrase

13. (May) sample

14. "The Race for the South Pole"

15. remains

16. complete sentence

17. alongside, through

18. a. noun
    b. pōl´ tis
    c. Latin

19. a. (p)neumonia
    b. woul(d)
    c. pi(t)ch

20. Example: Please bring some cheese. I am baking bread.

21. declarative

22. my, the, those, two, Ms. Hoo's

23. hushes

24. a. (is) denying
    b. denied
    c. (has) denied

25. rusty, old, shiny, new, compact, sporty, gigantic, powerful, classy, expensive

26. Ms. Hoo said, "My car was made in France, not in Japan."

27. a. leaves
    b. bison
    c. mouthfuls

28. Ms. Hoo | drove   I | walked

    friends | rode

29. ancestors | built | cabins
    My maternal   some rustic

30. ancestors | Did build | teepees
    Dan's paternal

LESSON 44 — Object of the Preposition • The Prepositional Phrase

Practice 44

a. around (us)
   in (some)
   of (us)

b. to (us)
   from (Washington)
   by (truck) and (train)

c. of the (Cascade Mountains)
   like a (desert)

d. Beyond the (shoreline)
   off (rocks)
   into the (ocean)

e. Prudent

f. Imprudent

More Practice 44

1. At (sunrise)
   at her (clock)
   about her (students)
   into her (car)

2. past a (house)
   with (daffodils)
   in the (yard)

3. Along the (way)
   at a (cow)
   in the (middle)
   of the (road)

4. to the (left)
   on the (right)

5. Near the (school)
   for (pedestrians)

6. Without (doubt)
   on (time)
   for (class)

Review Set 44

1. Paternal

2. waste

3. knowledge

4. touched

5. strength

6. plural

7. a. buried
   b. beautiful

8. a. topped
   b. referred

9. a. reign
   b. yield

10. Washington, American

11. Dear James,
    Please join me for dinner on Saturday. I shall serve Boston baked beans.
                                    Love,
                                    Ima

12. clause

13. (will) (be) flying

14. I believe Dr. Rhombus was Mother's geometry professor.

www.saxonhomeschool.com
©Houghton Mifflin Harcourt Publishers, Inc.
41
Grammar and Writing 5
Teacher Packet, 9781419098499

15. seemed

16. run-on sentence

17. With (ease)
    through the (door)
    down the (stairs)
    into the (basement)

18. a. intransitive verb
    b. ri sēd´
    c. Latin

19. a. edge
    b. guest
    c. high

20. Example: Washington, D.C., is our
    nation's capital.

21. throughout

22. a, few, Jasmin's, my, two, her

23. tried

24. a. (is) stopping
    b. stopped
    c. (has) stopped

25. rare, poisonous, slithery, slender, gigantic,
    strong, dangerous, hungry, harmless,
    friendly

26. I. Gopher snakes
       A. Where they live
       B. What they eat

27. a. waltzes
    b. pennies
    c. autos

28. trouble | starts   Ann | opens

    Rufus | escapes

29. cousin | eats | vegetables
    My prudent   many green

30. you | Have been eating | vegetables
                              your

LESSON 45   The Prepositional Phrase as an Adjective • Diagramming

Practice 45

a. picture

b. flag

c. friendship

d. *for you* describes "surprise"

e. *through the forest* describes "road"

f. malicious

g. Malice

h. Wally | likes | stories
                    about
                       spies

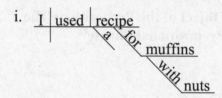

i. I | used | recipe
          a   for
               muffins
               with
                  nuts

Review Set 45

1. Prudent

2. Maternal

3. economical

4. synonyms

5. fire

6. abstract

7. a. fried
   b. sleepiness

8. a. matted
   b. preferred

9. a. belief
   b. weight

10. Scottish

11. Out in the wild West, a Baptist preacher
    read from the Holy Bible.

12. phrase

13. (should) (have) brought

14. "Adrift on an Ice Pan"

15. smell

16. complete sentence

17. For (fun)
    to my (friend)
    into a (bottle)
    into the (sea)

18. a. adjective
    b. rō tund´
    c. Latin

19. a. (wrist)
    b. (rh)ombus
    c. si(gh)

20. Example: We toured the White House, and then we saw the Jefferson and Lincoln Memorials.

21. imperative

22. her, Jasmin's, my, two

23. hisses

24. a. (is) multiplying
    b. multiplied
    c. (has) multiplied

25. delicious, buttery, dry, crumbly, sweet, sticky, gooey, vanilla-flavored, over-cooked, inedible

26. Jasmin asks, "Where are my Jerusalem crickets?"

27. a. public libraries
    b. apologies
    c. Tuesdays

28. Ms. Hoo | is shouting

    students | are searching

    pet | has disappeared

29.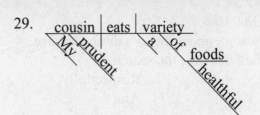

30.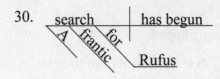

LESSON 46   Indirect Objects

Practice 46

a. Illiterate

b. Literate

c. him

d. owner

e. teams

f. no indirect object

g.   Ms. Hoo | read | poem
        \(x\) \ us

Review Set 46

1. Malice

2. prudent

3. father

4. wasteful

5. *ignis*

6. compound

7. a. gripping
   b. creepiest

8. Vivian

9. a. grief
   b. sleigh

10. Jerusalem

11. Dear Ms. Hoo,
    I am sorry about Rufus's disappearance.
    We shall continue the search.
                        Respectfully,
                        Ann

12. clause

13. (Could) (have) jumped

14. Did Deputy Jesse learn to fix flat tires in
    Dr. Funk's Latin class?

15. remains

16. complete sentence

17. under the (seat)
    of William's (bicycle)

18. a. adjective
    b. ar´ id
    c. Latin

19. a. door(k)nob
    b. s(c)ience
    c. a(dj)ective

20. Example: Are we hearing the song of a
    meadowlark?

21. beware

22. three, the, their, this

23. will find

24. a. (is) glorifying
    b. glorified
    c. (has) glorified

25. ridiculous, tall, magnificent, fuzzy, small,
    round, crazy, crooked, funny, square

26. A cat came fiddling out of a barn
    With a pair of bagpipes under her arm.

27. a. mothers-in-law
    b. peaches
    c. Wednesdays

28. Moses | empties   Rosa | moves

    students | squeal

29.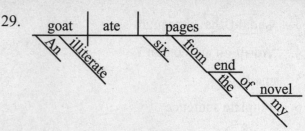

30.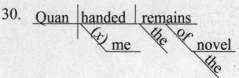

LESSON 47   The Period, Part 1

Practice 47

a. I. Rodeo competition
   A. Riding broncos
   B. Roping steer

b. J.B. Hoven wrote a novel called *The
   Bucking Bronco*.

c. Don't be ridiculous.

d. Eagles soar among the clouds.

e. momentary

f. momentous

More Practice 47   *See Master Worksheets*

Review Set 47

1. Literate

2. Malicious

3. unwise

4. mother

5. *Val-*

6. possessive

7. a. drying
   b. bigger

8. me

9. a. believing
   b. deceiving

10. Swiss, Russian

11. Black-collared lizards
    live in deserts of the Southwest.

12. phrase

13. (can) broaden

14. "On the Sunny Side of the Street"

15. grew

16. sentence fragment

17. at the (school)
    except the (principal)
    about this missing (pet)

18. a. noun
    b. bā′ lif
    c. Old French

19. a. wa(l)king
    b. s(c)ent
    c. ba(d)ge

20. I believe A. J. Gallo plays the violin.

21. interrogative

22. The, his, Ms. Hoo's, many

23. catches

24. a. (is) simplifying
    b. simplified
    c. (has) simplified

25. long, silly, serious, true, mysterious,
    imaginative, fictitious, humorous, dark,
    scary

26. The principal says, "A bearded dragon
    belongs in central Australia, not in a
    classroom."

27. a. fistfuls
    b. cherries
    c. trays

28.

29.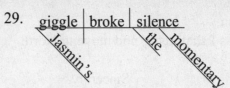

30.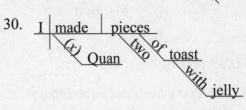

LESSON 48 Coordinating Conjunctions

Practice 48

a. and, or, for, so

b. but, nor, yet

c. listed above

d. and, but, and

e. or, nor

f. for, yet

g. so

h. plausible

i. implausible

Review Set 48

1. Momentary

2. read

3. evil

4. Prudent

5. strength

6. abstract

7. a. laid
   b. spinning

8. Dolly

9. a. briefcase
   b. their

10. and, but

11. Dear Ann,
    Perhaps I shall retire and move to North Dakota.
                                    Sincerely,
                                    Ms. Hoo

12. clause

13. (might) (be) passing

14. I think Officer Ambush has issued more speeding tickets than any other officer in the West.

15. sounds

16. complete sentence

17. Beside William's (chair)
    of (bread)
    amid (pieces)
    of torn (paper)

18. a. noun
    b. bi kwest′
    c. Old English

19. a. hand(s)ome
    b. chalk
    c. scene

20. Give my regards to Paul R. Flores.

21. hook

22. This, some, Florida, six

23. hummed

24. a. (is) humming
    b. hummed
    c. (has) hummed

25. malicious, sneaky, shy, timid, friendly, exuberant, generous, vivacious, quiet, serene

26. I. Thomas's hobbies
    A. Reading mysteries
    B. Riding bikes
    C. Playing the trumpet

27. a. children of the king
    b. hobbies
    c. trout

28.

29.

30.

LESSON 49 Diagramming Compound Subjects and Predicates

Practice 49

a. tolerable

b. intolerable

c.

d.

e.

More Practice 49 *See Master Worksheets*

Review Set 49

1. true

2. Momentous

3. read

4. harm

5. metamorphosis

6. collective

7. a. driest
    b. hopped

8. Sarah

9. a. piece
    b. beige

10. and, but, or, for, nor, yet, so

11. In October we enjoy fall colors in the Northeast.

12. phrase

13. (could) (have) run

14. *The Tales of Uncle Remus*

15. felt

16. run-on sentence

17. throughout the (classroom)
    around (books)
    under (desks)
    behind (cabinets)

18. a. adjective
    b. skant
    c. Middle English

19. a. (g)naw
    b. (w)rench
    c. solem(n)

20. Jack B. Nimble burned his toes.

21. interrogative

22. Those, Labrador, the, several

23. identifies

24. a. (is) identifying
    b. identified
    c. (has) identified

25. large, empty, small, dirty, clean, comfortable, spacious, elegant, expansive, sturdy

26. The principal complains, "This chaos is intolerable."

27. a. Labrador retrievers
    b. feet
    c. capfuls

28.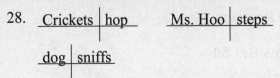

29.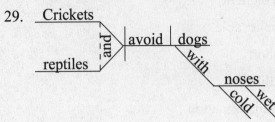

30.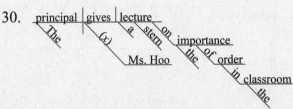

LESSON 50 The Period, Part 2: Abbreviations, Decimals

Practice 50

a. Mr. and Mrs. Hatti drove south on Baldwin Avenue. (3 periods)

b. School begins at 8 a.m. each weekday. (3 periods)

c. Ms. Lim winked at Ms. Hoo. (3 periods)

d. Rev. Freddy Rivas performed the marriage ceremony. (2 periods)

e. Capt. H. R. Montgomery commands the troops. (4 periods)

f. "Gimme Toy Co." was the name on the box. (2 periods)

g. Prof. Werks wrote, "Hike to Mt. Whitney in Aug." (3 periods)

h. We had driven 7.2 (seven and two tenths) miles. (2 periods)

i. benevolence

j. benevolent

Review Set 50

1. Tolerable

2. believable

3. short

4. Illiterate

5. transformation

6. possessive

7. a. patted
   b. cried

8. Aaron

9. a. receiver
   b. neighborly

10. or, so

11. Dear Ms. Hoo,
    The noise from your room disturbs my students.
    Respectfully,
    Mr. Annoyd

12. clause

13. (must) warn

14. Is Rufus attending Professor Speek's French class with Uncle Noah?

15. grew

16. sentence fragment

17. After (lunch)
    at the (clock)
    on her (desk)
    for thirty (minutes)

18. a. adjective
    b. lim´ pid
    c. French (from Latin)

19. a. cas(t)le
    b. s(c)ent
    c. shou(l)d

20. An ambulance rushed Mr. Jack B. Nimble to the Joan C. Giddy Hospital at seven p.m.

21. swell

22. One, Labrador, a, Perlina's

23. swatted

24. a. (is) swatting
    b. swatted
    c. (has) swatted

25. kind, helpful, patient, benevolent, compassionate, caring, strict, stern, friendly, passionate

26. Little Miss Muffet
    Sat on a tuffet…

27. a. men of God
    b. geese
    c. matches

28.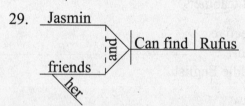

29.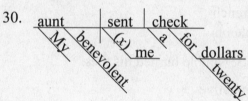

30.

LESSON 51   **The Predicate Nominative**

Practice 51

a. canine

b. feline

c. Lake Placid | became \ resort

d. Uncle Sam | was \ person

e. Jimmy Carter | became \ President

f. father | is \ Virginian

More Practice 51 *See "Corny Chronicle #3" in Master Worksheets*

Review Set 51

1. generous

2. intolerable

3. unlikely

4. important

5. delta

6. abstract

7. a. happiest
   b. bigger

8. Isabel

9. a. friend
   b. weighing

10. and, but, or, for, nor, yet, so

11. Mr. Annoyd would send the bearded dragon back to Central Australia.

12. phrase

13. (have)(been) picking

14. "There's a Hole in the Bucket"

15. character

16. complete sentence

17. During the (blizzard)
    into the (wind)
    toward (home)

18. a. noun
    b. nut´ hach
    c. Middle English

19. a. (knowing)
    b. a(che)
    c. bri(ght)

20. Dr. Payne will mail the bill to Mr. Jack B. Nimble, 531 Candlestick Rd.

21. smelled

22. A, Russian, the, Jasmin's

23. cherishes

24. a. (is) verifying
    b. verified
    c. (has) verified

25. worried, fretful, angry, resentful, sour, unfriendly, serious, no-nonsense, grouchy, unhappy, jolly, gracious, mischievous, sneaky

26. Mr. Annoyd says, "Please be quiet."

27. a. glasses of milk
    b. children
    c. glassfuls

28. principal | has gone

    secretary | will handle   she | is

29.
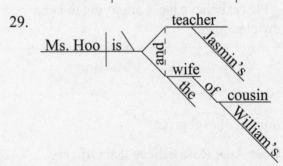

30. friends | are giving | headache
    Our canine (x) Mr. Annoyd a

LESSON 52   **Noun Case, Part 1: Nominative, Possessive**

Practice 52

a. nominative case; subject

b. nominative case; predicate nominative

c. possessive case

d. nominative case; subject

e. nominative case; predicate nominative

f. equine

g. bovine

Review Set 52

1. feline
2. Benevolent
3. bearable
4. antonyms
5. tributary
6. collective
7. a. merrily
   b. admitted
8. Esperanza
9. a. relief
   b. weighty
10. and, yet
11. Dear Mr. Annoyd,
    Please believe me. I am trying to keep my class quiet.

    Seriously,
    Ms. Hoo
12. clause
13. (might) (have) given
14. Does Aunt Rosa believe that Officer Ambush has an invisible car?
15. gift
16. sentence fragment
17. of (love)
    for the (land)
18. a. adjective
    b. mān´ jē
    c. Middle English
19. a. colum(n)
    b. ma(t)ch
    c. (who)
20. Ms. Hatti will begin teaching on Sept. 9.
21. interrogative
22. A, helpful, the, clear, glass

23. stirred
24. a. (is) stirring
    b. stirred
    c. (has) stirred
25. nominative case
26. I. Bovine animals
    A. Oxen
    B. Antelope
    C. Cows
27. a. science teachers
    b. oxen
    c. thieves
28. he | returns

    Mr. Stoneman | will visit

    she | has gone
29.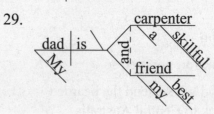
30.

LESSON 53   Noun Case, Part 2: Objective

Practice 53

a. O.P.
b. I.O.
c. D.O.
d. O.P.
e. D.O.
f. I.O.
g. nominative case

h. objective case

i. possessive case

j. objective case

k. auditory

l. olfactory

Review Set 53

1. horses

2. canine

3. good

4. Intolerable

5. hemisphere

6. plural

7. a. cries
   b. topping

8. fiddler

9. a. field
   b. conceit

10. and, but, or, for, nor, yet, so

11. In the Midwest, people attend rodeos for entertainment.

12. phrase

13. (will) (have) completed

14. Little House on the Prairie.

15. waterfall

16. run-on sentence

17. From the (city)
    of (Hershey)
    in (Pennsylvania)
    of the world's (chocolate)

18. a. noun
    b. mal´ is
    c. Old French (from Latin)

19. a. (k)nock
    b. lam(b)
    c. gu(e)ss

20. Dr. Jo B. Ngo will see you at two p.m. tomorrow.

21. wart

22. A, glorious, the, smooth, glacial

23. shall paint

24. a. (is) dipping
    b. dipped
    c. (has) dipped

25. objective case

26. Mr. Stoneman said, "Perhaps I shall cancel school until Friday."

27. a. birds of prey
    b. Fridays
    c. centuries

28. chaos | continues

    Mr. Stoneman | will cancel

    Ms. Hoo | captures

29.
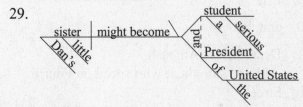

30.
Adam
and
Eva | sent | address
(x) | me | their new

LESSON 54 The Predicate Adjective

Practice 54

a. Bison | are \ plentiful

b. Beets
    and
    hay | have been \ profitable

c.

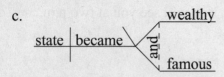

```
state | became \ <wealthy
                  and
                  >famous
```

d. Designers | were \ creative

e. Aboreal

f. amphibian

Review Set 54

1. olfactory

2. bovine

3. cat

4. Benevolent

5. Latitude

6. concrete

7. tried

8. neighbor, believes

9. Erik

10. and, but

11. Dear Officer Ambush
    Please stop those who speed on Fourth Street.
    Respectfully,
    Josef Habib

12. clause

13. (must) (have) seen

14. Esperanza desperately wants Grandma to join her.

15. hopeful

16. sentence fragment

17. From (dawn) until (dusk) in (baskets)

18. a. noun
    b. māz
    c. Spanish

19. a. (wreath)
    b. (adjust)
    c. (calf)

20. I. Cities in Delaware
    A. Wilmington—capital
    B. Lewes—whaling colony

21. interrogative

22. this, delicious, ripe, fertile

23. pries

24. a. (is) prying
    b. pried
    c. (has) pried

25. nominative case

26. No one can say
    What will happen today.

27. a. lunch breaks
    b. calves
    c. stories

28. Ms. Hoo | finds | she | will scold

    he | has caused

29.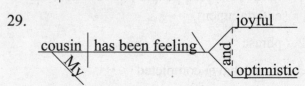

    ```
    cousin | has been feeling \ <joyful
      My                        and
                                >optimistic
    ```

30.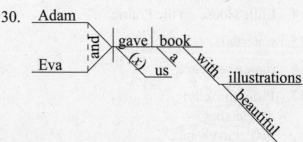

    ```
    Adam \
          and > gave | book
    Eva  /       (x) a
                 us   with illustrations
                          beautiful
    ```

LESSON 55   Comparison Adjectives

Practice 55

a. bigger, comparative

b. youngest, superlative

c. most, superlative

d. sleepier, comparative

e. cutest; superlative

f. faster; comparative

g. louder, loudest

h. more (or less) plausible
   most (or least) plausible

i. gentility

j. genteel

Review Set 55

1. land

2. auditory

3. cow

4. canine

5. longitude

6. collective

7. famous, funny

8. thieves, received, their

9. smaller

10. and, but, or, for, nor, yet, so

11. Many Quakers settled in the Northeast.

12. phrase

13. Tanner

14. *A New Dictionary of Quotations*

15. delicious

16. complete sentence

17. Throughout the (year)
    of (exercisers)
    on the (path)
    around the (park)

18. a. noun
    b. lin´ gwist
    c. Latin

19. a. could
    b. guide
    c. whose

20. Mario M. DeSurra provided these instructions: on Mon., Feb. 2, go west to Arrival St. to see the groundhog.

21. swell

22. The, frigid, blustery, watery, red

23. dried

24. a. (is) drying
    b. dried
    c. (has) dried

25. nominative case

26. Ms. Hoo said, "Please take your seats."

27. a. flower boxes
    b. shovelfuls
    c. bunches

28. Ms. Hoo | smiled   students | cheered

    Jasmin | found

29.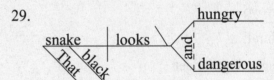

30. Adam
    and | baked | loaf
    Eva | (x) | a | of
    Ms. Hoo | bread

LESSON 56   Irregular Comparison Adjectives

Practice 56

a. Many

b. much

c. worst

d. More

e. Little

f. more scary

g. Indolent

h. Industrious

More Practice 56

1. Less

2. better

3. worst

4. better

5. more reliable

6. more

7. most benevolent

8. wiser

Review Set 56

1. polite

2. trees

3. smell

4. cattle

5. arroyo

6. plural

7. beginning, sadder

8. niece, beige

9. tallest

10. redder

11. Dear Mr. Stoneman,
    We have found one of the lost critters,
    but I do not know where the others are.
    Regretfully,
    Ms. Hoo

12. clause

13. nor, but, and

14. Professor U.R. Thair teaches history and
    Spanish.

15. spaghetti

16. run-on sentence

17. across the (United States)
    of (wheat)
    of (cattle)

18. a. noun
    b. links
    c. Middle English

19. a. (whole)
    b. sketch
    c. (hour)

20. Ms. Hoo wrote, "All assignments are due
    Fri., Apr. 21."

21. exclamatory

22. The, white, fluffy, small, long

23. polishes

24. a. (is) hopping
    b. hopped
    c. (has) hopped

25. objective case

26. I. Common pets
    A. Dogs
    B. Cats
    C. Birds

27. a. dog dishes
    b. handfuls
    c. sheep

28. Dogs | are sniffing

    students | are searching

    Rufus | is resting

29.

30.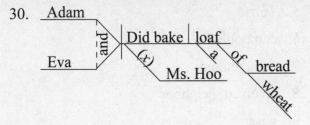

LESSON 57   The Comma, Part 1: Dates, Addresses, Series

Practice 57

a. providential

b. providence

c. Lily ran fast and broke the school record in the mile on Wednesday, December 7, 2005.

d. no comma needed

e. Christmas fell on Sunday, December 25, in the year 2005.

f. The post office has moved to 612 W. Duarte Road, Arcadia, California 91007.

g. Boise, Idaho, was Mr. Spud's birthplace.

h. Are you talking about Salem, Massachusetts, or Salem, Oregon?

i. The eight parts of speech include nouns, pronouns, verbs, adverbs, adjectives, prepositions, conjunctions, and interjections.

j. Lucy saw two gray squirrels, a blue jay, and three robins in the park.

More Practice 57   *See Master Worksheets*

Review Set 57

1. Industrious

2. gentility

3. amphibian

4. hearing

5. Capricorn

6. abstract

7. flies, biggest

8. believe, ceiling

9. taller

10. fewer

11. Dear Katy,
    Shall we play Chinese checkers after school?

    Your friend,
    Marta

12. phrase

13. Chris

14. "Bicycle Built for Two"

15. glorious

16. complete sentence

17. Inside a coal (mine)
    of (coal)
    on a (track)

18. a. adjective
    b. kyoo′ boid
    c. Greek

19. a. talk
    b. light
    c. gnat

20. Dr. Ngo's office has moved to 54 W. Main Street.

21. play

22. A, huge, brown, the, red

23. Lana was born on Sunday, November 4, 1973, in Detroit, Michigan.

24. a. (is) slamming
    b. slammed
    c. (has) slammed

25. possessive case

26. Nora asked, "May I help you?"

27. a. dog leashes
    b. babies
    c. wolves

28.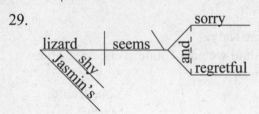
Ms. Hoo | thinks

Jasmin | should take

he | has caused

29.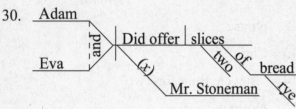

30.
Adam
and
Eva
Did offer | slices
two
of
bread
rye
(x)
Mr. Stoneman

LESSON 58 Appositives

Practice 58

a. Superfluous

b. supersonic

c. super

d. the capital of Georgia

e. cinnamon

f.   Ben Chu (artist) | draws | cartoons
        an

g. Ms. Hoo, my teacher, wants me to succeed.

h. Mr. Stoneman, principal of Giggly School, encourages students to try hard.

Review Set 58

1. providence

2. indolent

3. Genteel

4. tree

5. Torrid

6. compound

7. tries, matted

8. received, neighbor

9. wiser

10. fewer

11. Dear Ms. Hoo,
    Pets are not allowed at Mudvalley Middle School.
                          Regards,
                          Mr. Stoneman

12. clause

13. and, but, or, for, nor, yet, so

14. Did you, Auntie, call Dr. Rizkalla?

15. teacher

16. sentence fragment

17. Despite our (fatigue)
    against the strong (current)
    toward the distant (shore)

18. a. adjective
    b. krip´ tic
    c. Greek

19. the site of the first World Series

20. The bridge on First Ave. will be closed Dec. and Jan.

21. declarative

22. Two, gooey, the, their

23. Nancy raises cattle, sheep, chickens, and horses.

24. a. (is) replying
    b. replied
    c. (has) replied

25. objective case

26. Smile at your troubles
    And pop them like bubbles.

27. a. watch dogs
    b. earfuls
    c. candies

28.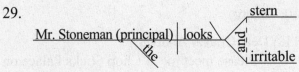

Jasmin | says

dogs | caused

Rufus | was

29.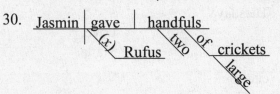

Mr. Stoneman (principal) | looks \ stern \ and \ irritable / the

30. Jasmin | gave | handfuls
(x) Rufus | two of crickets large

LESSON 59   The Comma, Part 2: Direct Address and Academic Degrees

Practice 59

a. Baukien, we learned a new song yesterday.

b. Please remember, my dear friends, that I shall return soon.

c. Carrie Prince, R.N., cares for newborn babies.

d. My cat's health is very important to Carla Wheat, D.V.M.

e. *lumen*

f. illuminate

g. Luminous

More Practice 59   *See Master Worksheets*

Review Set 59

1. super
2. fortunate
3. hard-working
4. polite
5. savanna
6. plural
7. winner, famous

8. chief, receive
9. friendliest
10. fewer
11. On a humid afternoon in the South, my cousins gather at the northeast corner of the park to play checkers.
12. phrase
13. Chris
14. "When Icicles Hang by the Wall."
15. energetic
16. run-on sentence
17. For this (assignment) of the (states) on the (walls) around the (room)
18. a. (wrinkle)
    b. calm
19. Nevada, the "silver state," borders five other states.
20. On Thurs. at nine a.m., I shall attend a lecture on the life of Dr. Martin L. King.
21. fleeing
22. a, generous, the, ugly
23. Ms. Hoo, have you seen my lunch, my backpack, or my history book?
24. a. (is) smiling
    b. smiled
    c. (has) smiled
25. objective case
26. Mr. Stoneman replied, "No, Jasmin, I have not fired your teacher."
27. a. topic sentences
    b. rose bushes
    c. Jennys

28.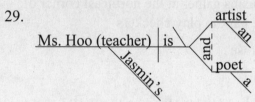

Jasmin | is weeping

Mr. Stoneman | says

Rufus | must go

29.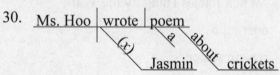

30. Ms. Hoo | wrote | poem

LESSON 60   The Comma, Part 3: Appositives

Practice 60

a. Chris—an essential appositive

b. "the girl with black silky hair"—a nonessential appositive

c. Hans Christian Andersen, author of "The Princess and the Pea," wrote many entertaining stories for children.

d. no commas needed, essential appositive

e. Dr. May, the town's only physician, is busy during flu season.

f. no commas needed, essential appositive

g. inopportune

h. opportune

More Practice 60 *See Master Worksheets*

Review Set 60

1. *lumen*

2. greater

3. Providence

4. Indolent

5. plateau

6. abstract

7. cries, biggest

8. friend, freight

9. quieter

10. many

11. Dear Cousin Anabel,
    Please meet me at Chop Sticks Palace on Tuesday.
               Love,
               Marta

12. clause

13. or, so

14. Why, Dr. Mejares, must I study a foreign language?

15. violinist

16. complete sentence

17. out the (door)
    down the (street)
    to the (post office)

18. a. noun
    b. hej
    c. Old English

19. My father, Mr. Curtis, can repair your broken computer.

20. Were Mr. and Mrs. Hahn married on Mt. Wilson?

21. imperative

22. the, mature, gentle, the, white, my, two

23. I spoke with Ann Wong, R.N., on Monday, January 2, 2006.

24. a. (is) pitying
    b. pitied
    c. (has) pitied

25. nominative case

26. I. Crops in Iowa
    A. Corn
    B. Oats
    C. Soybeans

27. a. journal entries
     b. cans of corn
     c. truckfuls

28. Rufus | leaves

     critters | will miss

     he | is

29.
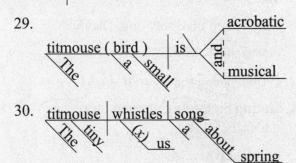
The titmouse (bird) is a small and acrobatic musical

30.
The tiny titmouse (x) whistles a song us about spring

LESSON 61 — Overused Adjectives • Unnecessary Articles

Practice 61 *Answers will vary.*

   a. foul, stormy, dreary, foggy, miserable

   b. interesting, thoughtful, entertaining

   c. pretty, glamorous, lovely, stylish

   d. old, sour, foul, spoiled

   e. That sort of bug frightens me.

   f. The babies were tired, so we put both of them to bed.

   g. Intuition

   h. Intuitive

Review Set 61

1. Opportune

2. light

3. Supersonic

4. care

5. Its

6. collective

7. gently, sadder

8. their, beliefs

9. quietest

10. fewer

11. Do citrus trees grow in the West?

12. phrase

13. Rosella

14. *The Heart of a Chief*

15. delightful and educational

16. B (unnecessary article "the" in sentence A)

17. Down the (hill;) across the (meadow)

18. a. scissors
     b. pnemonia
     c. through

19. Mr. Cabrera, my next-door neighbor, owns a Mexican restaurant in Los Angeles.

20. Dr. Y. I. Knap rests each day at two p.m.

21. cook

22. Ambitious, tiny, the, versatile, popular

23. Dr. Chu, you have an appointment with Thomas Curtis, M.B.A., on Tuesday, January 2, 2007.

24. a. (is) begging
     b. begged
     c. (has) begged

25. objective case

26. Miss Fortune asked, "Have you seen my purse?"

27. a. trenches
     b. human rights
     c. dishfuls

28. Rufus | cries

     nose | runs

     he | gets

29.

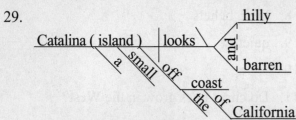

30.

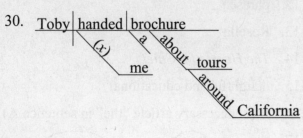

LESSON 62   Pronouns and Antecedents

Practice 62

a. Opal

b. Juan

c. Clem, Violet; llamas

d. umbrella

e. While Elle and Amelia were waiting, Elle wrote her essay.

f. The engine sputtered and coughed.

g. cowardice

h. intrepid

Review Set 62

1. Intuition

2. bad

3. shining

4. above

5. high

6. possessive

7. happiest, smiling

8. relieved, neighbor

9. quieter

10. quietest

11. Dear Mrs. Roper,
    I wish to commend your intrepid assistant for capturing the run-away cheetah last Wednesday.
    Gratefully,
    Mr. Perez

12. purse

13. and

14. May I keep this stray dog, Daddy?

15. electrician

16. B (unnecessary article "a" in A)

17. During the (storm;) around the (room;) under the (sofa)

18. a. adjective
    b. hek´ tik
    c. Greek

19. Rosa's youngest sister, Violeta, has chickenpox.

20. Mr. Dew now lives on S. Olive St. in Sacramento.

21. imperative

22. A, smelly, mangy, stray, the, her

23. Mora, we were on vacation in Oskaloosa, Iowa.

24. a. (is) steadying
    b. steadied
    c. (has) steadied

25. possessive case

26. Cut thistles in May,
    They'll grow in a day…

27. a. Gomezes
    b. waltzes
    c. women

28. horses | stomp

    cows | moo

    Olaf | delivers

29.

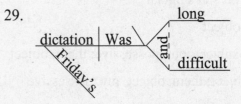
（diagram: Today's / weather | appears / in / Pennsylvania / but / sunny / cold）

30.

（diagram: P. Phil (groundhog) | gave | prediction / a / famous / (x) / his / us / concerning / winter）

LESSON 63   The Comma, Part 4: Greetings and Closings, Last Name First

Practice 63

a. Dear Tyrell,
   Thank you… "Abram, Peter."
           Gratefully,
           Hepzy

b. The index… "Carroll, Lewis" ….

c. Tenacity

d. Tenacious

Review Set 63

1. fearless

2. intuition

3. well-timed

4. Luminous

5. placate

6. abstract

7. funny, daily

8. deceive, chief

9. redder

10. reddest

11. Dear Mrs. Roper,
   I appreciate your tenacity in arguing my case in court on Thursday.
           Gratefully,
           Mr. Perez

12. phrase

13. Gertrude

14. *Because of Winn-Dixie*

15. clean, attractive

16. Examples: captivating, encouraging, inspiring

17. about (you;) since (Tuesday)

18. a. adjective
    b. si fal′ ik
    c. Greek

19. Pewny, my youngest cousin, eats my broccoli for me.

20. The dog's collar costs $2.50 (two dollars and fifty cents).

21. is

22. a, shimmery, green

23. Luis, you may pick up your order on Monday, Wednesday, or Friday.

24. a. (is) tapping
    b. tapped
    c. (has) tapped

25. nominative case

26. Inez asked, "Who spilled the paint?"

27. a. sea serpents
    b. sheep
    c. thieves

28. Lily | made

    she | did

    she | has been studying

29.

（diagram: Friday's / dictation | Was / long / and / difficult）

30.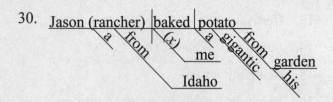

LESSON 64   Personal Pronouns

Practice 64

a. Unethical

b. Ethical

c. me, first person

d. He, third person

e. you, second person

f. us, plural

g. me, singular

h. subject

i. direct object

j. indirect object

k. possession

More Practice 64

1. we, first person plural; you, second person singular or plural

2. they, third person plural

3. him, third person singular

4. They, third person plural; their, third person plural; it, third person singular

5. you, second person singular or plural; my, first person singular

6. her, object

7. We, subject; our, possessive; them, object

8. I, subject; them, object; my, possessive

9. They, subject; me, object

10. She, subject; us, object

Review Set 64

1. Tenacious

2. Cowardice

3. knowledge

4. inopportune

5. calm

6. compound

7. mopped, dried

8. friend, field

9. many

10. first, singular

11. Dear Mr. Perez

    I shall represent you in the Philadelphia courthouse as long as your behavior remains ethical.

              Sincerely,

              Mrs. Roper

12. Miss Fortune

13. or

14. My mother, Dr. Ting Lacy, studied Latin.

15. today

16. sentence fragment

17. in the (corner;) opposite (Harry;) for two (hours)

18. br(i)dge

19. Chester, the biggest cat on the farm, is disturbing the hens.

20. Mrs. Ross gave us these directions: Go north to Vista St. and turn right.

21. declarative

22. clause

23. Boise, Idaho, will be my destination, John.

24. a. (is) supplying
    b. supplied
    c. (has) supplied

25. object

26. I. New hospital staff
   A. Dr. Eric Koesno
   B. Ms. Cherry Clegg, R.N.

27. a. can openers
   b. wolves
   c. radios

28.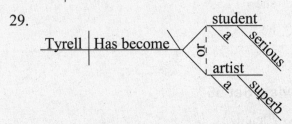

29.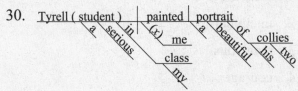

30. Tyrell (student) | painted | portrait

LESSON   Irregular Verbs, Part 2
65

Practice 65

a. elation

b. elated

c. blew

d. worn

e. sang

f. spoken

g. tore

h. known

i. stole

j. rung

k. grew, grown

l. bore, borne

m. rang, rung

n. sank, sunk

o. sang, sung

p. drank, drunk

q. chose, chosen

r. broke, broken

s. wore, worn

t. knew, known

u. blew, blown

v. began, begun

w. swore, sworn

x. spoke, spoken

Review Set 65

1. Ethical

2. tenacity

3. Intrepid

4. instinctive

5. bottom

6. plural

7. beginning, worrisome

8. perceives, achieved

9. better

10. first, plural

11. Dear Uncle Sergio,
   You can find her information in the directory under Blackly, Doris.
                    Your niece,
                    Daniela

12. boy

13. Lily

14. *The Sound of Music*

15. majestic

16. Examples: relaxing, exciting, fun

17. toward the ripest (tomato) on the (vine)

18. a. verb
   b. di lo͞od´
   c. Middle English (from Latin)

19. Marigold, a spotted mare, likes to gallop through the mud.

20. At one a.m. Ms. Overwork tore up her essay and began again.

21. swell

22. phrase

23. I shall see you, John, on Tuesday, January 16, 2007.

24. a. (is) blowing
    b. blew
    c. (has) blown

25. subject

26. A man of words and not of deeds
    Is like a garden full of weeds.

27. a. eyelashes
    b. bagfuls
    c. sopranos

28.

29.

30.

LESSON 66   Nominative Pronoun Case

Practice 66

a. Refer to the chart in Example 1

b. They are excellent writers.

c. The best writer was he.

d. Contrite

e. Contrition

f. She and I wore green

g. I, she, they, he, we

h. she

i. she

j. he

k. I

Review Set 66

1. Elated

2. unethical

3. tenacious

4. courage

5. Sedimentary

6. abstract

7. preferred, sunnier

8. weigh, piece

9. fewer

10. second

11. Dear Aunt Beki,
    Can you come to Mother's birthday party on Monday, May 5?
                    Your niece,
                    Daniela

12. purse

13. and, and, but

14. Leonard learned all about geology from his father, Dr. Trent, but nothing about English.

15. president

16. sentence fragment

17. With Yosemite's (Half Dome)
    in the (background)
    of our long (hike)
    to the (falls)

18. g(u)ide

19. My littlest brother, Andrew, found a worm
    in his apple.

20. On Dec. 24, 1914, Mr. John Muir died at
    the age of seventy-six.

21. he

22. clause

23. Jacob, I would like you to meet Yin Yu,
    D.D.S.

24. a. (is) bearing
    b. bore
    c. (has) borne

25. object

26. Hector said, "This purse belongs to the
    woman who stepped off the bus at Oak
    Street."

27. a. cups of tea
    b. cupfuls
    c. altos

28. Bozo | yipped

    he | saw

    she | is

29.
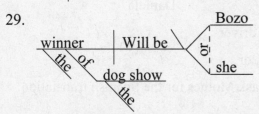

30.
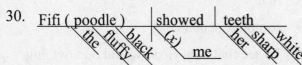

Practice 67

a. Yes, I speak English.

b. Of course, not everyone does.

c. His grandfather, I believe, came from
   Denmark.

d. The camel, it is said, has no sense of
   humor.

e. pertinent

f. irrelevant

More Practice 67 *See Master Worksheets*

Review Set 67

1. Contrite

2. high

3. Ethical

4. tenacious

5. caldera

6. possessive

7. fries, flattest

8. briefcase, conceited

9. worst

10. third, singular

11. Dear Daniela,
    Yes, I shall come to your mother's party
    on Monday, May 5.
    Love,
    Aunt Beki

12. Miss Fortune

12. us

14. *The Red Pony*

15. passionate

16. A (unnecessary article "The" in B)

17. With a (child)
    in a (backpack)
    to the (top)
    of (Sentinel Dome)

18. (two)

19. Ms. Hoo flew to Sacramento, the capital of California.

20. Dr. Kraning will lecture on Aug. 14.

21. I

22. phrase

23. If you have time, Mark, please bake two potatoes, some rolls, and a pie.

24. a. (is) beginning
    b. began
    c. (has) begun

25. subject

26. I. National parks
    A. Yosemite
    B. Yellowstone

27. a. pennies
    b. boxes of cereal
    c. trout

28. Fifi | growled   she | thought

    he | was

29.
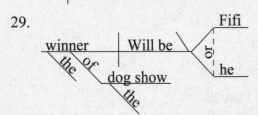

30.
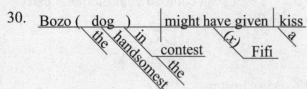

Practice 68

a. To Karen, Joyce meant trouble.

b. While passing, the driver honked.

c. After John, Thomas will speak.

d. Ornithology

e. Meteorology

Review Set 68

1. Pertinent

2. regret

3. high

4. Unethical

5. volcano's

6. interrogative

7. shopping, beautiful

8. receive, priest's

9. worse

10. third, plural

11. Dear Aunt Beki,
    Please bring paper plates, cups, and napkins to Mom's party, all right?
                    Many thanks,
                    Daniela

12. bus driver

13. and, or

14. I'll ask Mother for the Spanish translation.

15. rich

16. complete sentence

17. To see that dog, Bozo would do anything.

18. a. noun
    b. dē′ toor
    c. French (from Latin)

19. Ms. Hoo, a middle-school teacher, needs a vacation.

20. At one p.m. Mrs. Sizzle arrived in Death Valley.

21. she

22. clause

23. When you come, Ms. Hoo, please plan to stay until Friday, August 12.

24. a. (is) choosing
    b. chose
    c. (has) chosen

25. object

26. Fuzzy Wuzzy was a bear,
    Fuzzy Wuzzy had no hair,
    So Fuzzy Wuzzy wasn't fuzzy,
    Was he?

27. a. Rufuses
    b. French fries
    c. leashes

28. Bozo | yipped   he | thought

    she | was

29.

    Bozo | Has proved   faithful
                    and
                         obedient

30.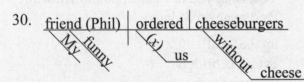
    friend (Phil) | ordered | cheeseburgers
    My funny (x) us without cheese

LESSON 69   Objective Pronoun Case

Practice 69

a. Refer to the chart in Example 1.

b. The noise frightened her.

c. Jesse sang me a song.

d. He has sung to us. *(Also correct: To us he has sung.)*

e. unfeigned

f. feign

g. Don't forget him or me.

h. me, him, them, her, us

i. him

j. him

k. me

Review Set 69

1. Irrelevant

2. Meteorology

3. sorry

4. Elation

5. meteorite

6. plural

7. objective

8. thief, freight

9. fewer

10. third, singular

11. Dear Peter,
    As I remember, your maternal ancestors are listed under Hillborne, Winona.
    Warmly,
    Uncle Jakob

12. telephone

13. Dara

14. "The Velveteen Rabbit"

15. tree

16. A (unnecessary article "a" in B)

17. To Elle, Gabriel seems indispensable.

18. (k)nee

19. Puerto Rico, a U.S. territory, has beautiful rain forests.

20. Mr. Lee N. Chen sent us to 142 E. Ash Ave.

21. subject

22. phrase

23. On June 26, 2008, I shall be eighty-six, my dear.

24. a. (is) knowing
    b. knew
    c. (has) known

25. me

26. Jasmin said, "We shall miss Ms. Hoo."

27. a. butterflies
    b. dollar bills
    c. peaches

28.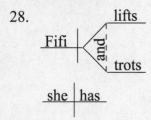

29.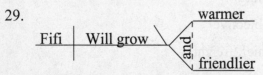

30.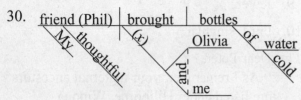

LESSON 70   Personal Pronoun Case Forms

Practice 70

a. objective case

b. nominative case

c. possessive case

d. objective of preposition

e. subject

f. direct object

g. indirect object

h. possession

i. they

j. me

k. linguistics

l. linguist

Review Set 70

1. Ornithology

2. Unfeigned

3. relevant

4. Contrition

5. meteor

6. concrete

7. nominative

8. trotted, steadily

9. prettiest

10. first, singular

11. Dear Uncle Jakob,
    I found my maternal ancestors, my paternal ancestors, and my lost library card.
    With gratitude,
    Peter

12. Juan

13. or, but

14. Yes, Dad, you have an appointment with Dr. Payne on Monday.

15. up the (trail)
    over the (bridge)
    through the (woods)

16. sentence fragment

17. Soon after, Ben fell asleep.

18. a. noun
    b. sī′ klōn
    c. Greek

19. Colorado, the Centennial State, is known for its many high mountain peaks.

20. Col. Robert Andrews has moved to St. Louis, Missouri.

21. she

22. clause

23. Professor Gomez, Ph.D., teaches English, French, and poetry.

24. a. (is) tearing
    b. tore
    c. (has) torn

25. B

26. I. The old railroad
    A. Steam trains
    B. Jenny railcars

27. a. solos
    b. sisters-in-law
    c. children

28.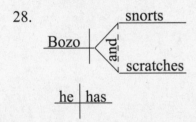

he | has

29.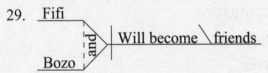

30.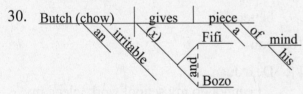

LESSON 71   Diagramming Pronouns

Practice 71

a. ardent

b. ardor

c.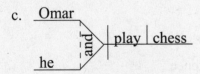

d.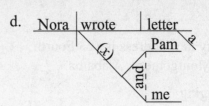

e.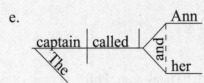

Review Set 71

1. Linguistics

2. feign

3. weather

4. relevant

5. Vertebrate

6. collective

7. objective

8. achieve, their

9. many

10. first, plural

11. Dear Quan,
    The deadline is Monday, May 10, 2010.
    Sincerely,
    Juan

12. bus

13. parks

14. "Look for the Silver Lining"

15. oak

16. Examples: faithful, reliable, cheerful

17. As you know, everything needs cleaning.

18. walk

19. Kansas, the Sunflower State, has prairies, farms, and rolling hills.

20. Mr. Thomas Cross, Jr., works for Barrons, Inc., in St. Louis.

21. subject

22. phrase

23. Egbert, my new address is 123 Fourth Avenue, Montgomery, Alabama.

24. a. (is) ringing
    b. rang
    c. (has) rung

25. her

26. Olivia said, "Thank you, Phil."

27. a. wrenches
    b. lawn mowers
    c. daisies

28.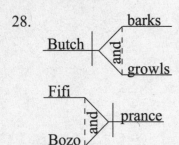

29.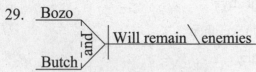

30.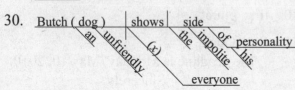

LESSON 72   Possessive Pronouns and Possessive Adjectives

Practice 72

a. its

b. their

c. hers

d. your

e. ours

f. serene

g. serenity

More Practice 72

1. their

2. They're

3. its

4. ours

5. hers

6. yours

7. your

8. It's, its

Review Set 72

1. linguist

2. Ardor

3. sincere

4. birds

5. vertebrate

6. interrogative

7. possessive

8. Your

9. better

10. you

11. Dear Juan,
    I cannot do my school work, clean my room, and meet your deadline.
                    Regretfully,
                    Quan

12. Juan

13. jay

14. Her classes include mathematics, Latin, biology, and English.

15. a. clapped
    b. glorious

16. run-on sentence

17. Because of Clark, Kent was late.

18. a. verb
    b. delv
    c. Middle English

19. Hawaii, the Aloha State, was formed by volcanic eruptions.

20. Ms. Hoo's note reads, "Homework due Fri., Feb. 3."

21. I

22. clause

23. No, Egbert, I did not move to Little Rock, Arkansas.

24. a. (is) freezing
    b. froze
    c. (has) frozen

25. A

26. Twinkle, twinkle, little star,
    How I wonder what you are…

27. a. patches
    b. dictionaries
    c. basketfuls

28.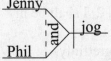

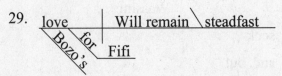

29.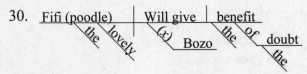

30. Fifi (poodle) | Will give | benefit | of doubt
    the lovely (x) Bozo the the

LESSON 73   Dependent and Independent Clauses • Subordinating Conjunctions

Practice 73

a. dependent

b. independent

c. independent

d. dependent

e. Unless

f. even though

g. When

h. sagacity

i. Sagacious

More Practice 73 *See Master Worksheets*

Review set 73

1. Serene

2. passionate

3. linguistics

4. pretend

5. valuable

6. possessive

7. nominative

8. yours

9. best

10. third, singular

11. Dear Cousin Wassim,
    Please come to my piano recital on Monday, April 2, 2008, at Grandmother's house.
                Your cousin,
                Aleda

12. Ms. Hoo

13. around the campground
    for bear-proof lockers
    for our food

14. while

15. a. trapped
    b. cloudiness

16. A

17. The day after, I mopped the floor.

18. flight

19. Moe, the smallest boy on the team, won the cross-country race last Saturday.

20. Capt. Rice lives on E. Sunshine Blvd. in St. Petersburg.

21. object

22. dependent

23. Luey, you may speak with Professor Grin, Ph.D., tomorrow.

24. a. (is) throwing
    b. threw
    c. (has) thrown

25. me

26. Carl said, "You should paint the room mustard yellow."

27. a. lives
    b. Fridays
    c. parties

28.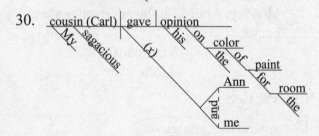

29.

30.

LESSON 74
The Comma, Part 7: Descriptive Adjectives, Dependent Clauses

Practice 74

a. We could hardly see through the deep, dense fog.

b. I took my biggest, warmest jacket to Minnesota, but ….

c. When … store, get a few peaches.

d. If they look bruised, buy ….

e. As soon … home, we'll ….

f. Redundancy

g. redundant

More Practice 74 *See Master Worksheets*

Review Set 74

1. Sagacious

2. peace

3. passion

4. language

5. asset

6. abstract

7. objective

8. hers

9. fewer

10. third, singular

11. Dear Cousin Aleda,
     On Monday, April 2, I shall be in Montpelier, Vermont.
                    Regretfully,
                    Wassim

12. sock

13. and, but

14. After

15. a. tapping
    b. penniless

16. complete sentence

17. To Omar, Nicasio appears malicious.

18. a. noun
    b. plum´ it
    c. Middle English (from Middle French)

19. Wyoming, the Equality State, has rugged mountains and windy flatlands.

20. He works at the Wumpit Toy Co., 12 N. Main St., Alhambra, CA

21. she

22. independent

23. If you go to Alaska, you might meet a huge, friendly moose.

24. a. (is) wearing
    b. wore
    c. (has) worn

25. her

26. I. Lakes
    A. Scenic views
    B. Water sports
    C. Houseboats

27. a. opportunities
    b. police chiefs
    c. knives

28.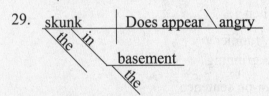

29.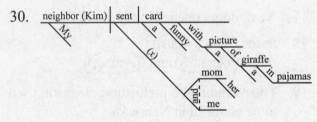

30.

LESSON 75   Compound Sentences • Coordinating Conjunctions

Practice 75

a. simple

b. compound; but

c. compound; and, so

d. simple

e. compound; for

f.

g. insatiable

h. satiable

Review Set 75

1. Redundant

2. Sagacity

3. peaceful

4. passionate

5. asset

6. collective

7. possessive

8. theirs

9. faster

10. third, plural

11. Dear Mrs. Cruz,
    My new address is 12 Sun Avenue, Frankfort, Kentucky.
                        Sincerely,
                        Mrs. Otto

12. compound

13. geyser

14. as

15. a. sleigh
    b. view

16. Examples: helpful, considerate, patient

17. With Dan, Smith can accomplish much.

18. bough

19. Tyrell, a tennis champion, is learning to play chess.

20. Dr. Norris's note reads, "Every 45 to 90 min., Old Faithful erupts."

www.saxonhomeschool.com
©Houghton Mifflin Harcourt Publishers, Inc.
73
Grammar and Writing 5
Teacher Packet, 9781419098499

21. object

22. phrase

23. When I swept the basement, I found a sneaky, stinky skunk.

24. a. (is) shrinking
    b. shrank
    c. (has) shrunk

25. B

26. Ivy said, "The goat is nibbling my ponytail!"

27. a. liberties
    b. wishes
    c. flower pots

28.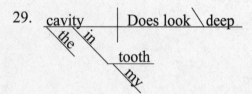

29.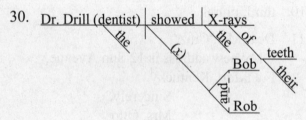

30. Dr. Drill (dentist) showed X-rays

h. "I … picture," she added.

i. quaintness

j. quaint

More Practice 76 *See Master Worksheets*

Review Set 76

1. Satiable

2. repetition

3. wise

4. synonyms

5. panacea

6. exclamatory

7. nominative

8. ours

9. many

10. first, plural

11. "Oh, the Places You'll Go"

12. door

13. temperature

14. when

15. a. funnier
    b. grinning

16. run-on sentence

17. Next, doors opened everywhere.

18. in the earth's (crust) through (cracks) and (fissures)

19. The mammoth, a prehistoric elephant, used to be plentiful in Nebraska.

20. Mr. and Mrs. Celoni took a nine a.m. flight to Memphis.

21. he

22. dependent

23. Mia said, "I read the lesson, but I did not understand it."

LESSON 76   **The Comma, Part 8: Compound Sentences, Direct Quotations**

Practice 76

a. and, but, or, nor, for, yet, so

b. for

c. yet

d. but

e. The lake was dry, and ….

f. Deer came for water, but ….

g. Mary said, "I've …."

24. a. (is) speaking
     b. spoke
     c. (has) spoken

25. me

26. and, but, or, for, nor, yet, so

27. a. eyeteeth
     b. toothbrushes
     c. team captains

28.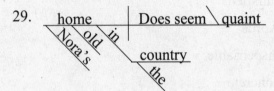
Egbert | is writing

Ivy | is playing

29.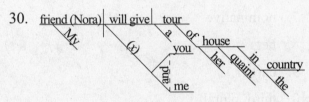

30.

LESSON 77   Relative Pronouns

Practice 77

a. who

b. who

c. whomever

d. that

e. whom

f. who | is \ friend
         my   best

g. ameliorate

h. amelioration

More Practice 77

1. who

2. who

3. whom

4. whom

5. whom

6. who

Review Set 77

1. old-fashioned

2. satisfied

3. wordy

4. wisdom

5. all

6. possessive

7. nominative

8. Your

9. fewer

10. first, plural

11. whom

12. simple

13. magnificent

14. because

15. a. pieces
     b. eight

16. B

17. Without Mia, Curtis is defenseless.

18. taught

19. Jerusalem crickets, scary-looking bugs, are not poisonous.

20. Mrs. Lowe's baby, James L. Ditter, Jr., weighs 27 lbs., 3 oz.

21. subject

22. phrase

23. As I stepped outside, I nearly squashed the biggest, ugliest bug on the planet.

24. a. (is) growing
     b. grew
     c. (has) grown

25. A

26. Ivy is playing games, for she has finished her essay.

27. Dear Anabel,
    Please call, write, or e-mail me soon.
                    Love,
                    Uncle Rigo

28.
    Ivy | is playing

    she | has finished

29.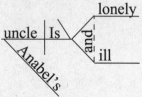
    uncle | Is \ lonely
          \ and
    Anabel's \ ill

30. Anabel (vocalist) | could sing | song
    an excellent (x) uncle a about
    her vacation in Maine her

LESSON 78 Pronoun Usage

Practice 78

a. We

b. us

c. us

d. I

e. we

f. salinity

g. saline

More Practice 78

1. he

2. We

3. us

4. she

5. her

6. he

7. she

8. they

9. We

10. us

Review Set 78

1. ameliorate

2. Quaintness

3. satisfied

4. words

5. dispensable

6. concrete

7. nominative

8. hers

9. curlier

10. third, plural

11. who

12. We

13. and, but, or, for, nor, yet, so

14. that

15. people

16. sentence fragment

17. From the sun, people were burned.

18. a. verb or noun
    b. di sper´
    c. Middle English (from Latin)

19. Missouri, the Show Me State, lies in the center of the continent.

20. The Atlas Tile Co. is located on S. Third St. in Rock City.

21. she

22. independent

23. As Olaf rode a white Arabian horse, Sven played a shiny, loud trumpet.

24. a. (is) swearing
    b. swore
    c. (has) sworn

25. her

26. Leo is playing games, but he hasn't won any.

27. *A Light in the Attic*

28.
```
hair | has shrunk
─────┼──────────
  he | washed
```

29.
```
we | shall call | Whom
```

30.
```
Buzz (barber) | Did give | haircut
   the           (x) Alex    a   short
```

LESSON 79   Interrogative Pronouns

Practice 79

a. what

b. none (*which* is an adjective)

c. Whose

d. Whom

e. Whose

f. Who

g. interrogative pronoun

h. adjective

i. daunt

j. dauntless

More Practice 79

1. Who's

2. Whose

3. Who

4. whom

5. Whom

6. Who's

7. Whose

8. whom

9. Who

10. Whom

Review Set 79

1. Saline

2. better

3. old

4. satisfied

5. essential

6. compound

7. objective

8. Their

9. curliest

10. second

11. whom

12. us

13. Whom

14. until

15. compound sentence

16. Who

17. This, Walter can do.

18. unfeigned

19. Arizona, the Grand Canyon State, gets very little rain.

20. They took water, fruit, cheese, etc., on their hike up Mt. Wilson.

21. object

22. except (Joe)
    alongside the (stream)

23. When Ms. Hoo retires, she will move to a quaint, small town.

24.
   a. (is) singing
   b. sang
   c. (has) sung

25. B

26. Yoli said, "I was born on Sunday, November 4, 1973, so how old am I?"

27. Dear Uncle Rigo,
       If you would like, I could bring you some bread, cheese, and grapes.
                          Love,
                          Anabel

28.

29.

30.

LESSON 80   Quotation Marks, Part 1

Practice 80

   a. none

   b. none

   c. "Inch by inch, … cinch," said Ms. Hoo.

   d. "If … time," said the teacher, "you'll … work."

   e. docent

   f. curator

More Practice 80 *See Master Worksheets*

Review Set 80

1. daunt

2. saltiness

3. improvement

4. Quaint

5. Indispensable

6. declarative

7. possessive

8. Whose

9. fewer, he

10. first, singular

11. who

12. We

13. Who

14. Whenever

15. sheep

16. quaint

17. For that, Sven paid forty dollars.

18.
   a. noun
   b. īs´ burg
   c. Danish, or Norwegian

19. Minnesota, the Gopher State, borders Lake Superior.

20. The note says, "Come to the library on Sat., Feb. 12."

21. he

22. dependent

23. "I like my students," said Ms. Hoo, "but their animals can be difficult."

24.
   a. (is) breaking
   b. broke
   c. (has) broken

25. her

26. I. Bryce National Park
       A. Geology
       B. Paleontology

27. Dear Anabel,
       I do not like bread and cheese, nor do I like grapes.
                          Thanks anyway,
                          Uncle Rigo

28. sheep | has broken

    Miss BoPeep | must carry

29. Miss BoPeep | should notify | Whom

30.

LESSON 81 Quotation Marks, Part 2

Practice 81

a. culprit

b. culpable

c. Have … "King Stork" by Howard Pyle?

d. Can … "Over the Rainbow" for me?

e. The … "Gone is Gone" comes from Bohemia.

f.   "Sit here, Molly, and tell me all about yourself. What are your hobbies?"
    "I like to catch butterflies and draw pictures," Molly said.

More Practice 81 *See Master Worksheets*

Review Set 81

1. docent

2. discouraged

3. salty

4. better

5. outcry

6. possessive

7. possessive

8. yours

9. fewest

10. first, plural

11. whom

12. we

13. whom

14. As soon as

15. simple sentence

16. Whom

17. That, Alba can take with her.

18. apologies

19. Badchek, the culprit, has fled to another country.

20. Mr. and Mrs. Tran live at 654 S. Alta Loma Dr. in Austin.

21. subject

22. Jenny replied, "No, I have not seen Badchek."

23. "If I see a suspicious, malicious person," said Jenny, "I shall call the police."

24. a. (is) drinking
    b. drank
    c. (has) drunk

25. Let us hum the song "The Old Gray Mare."

26. Fido eats my pizza, yet I forgive him.

27. Dear Officer Valiant,

    Your mean, avaricious culprit has lived in Iceland, Belgium, and Botswana.

       Respectfully,
       Mrs. Brite, P.I.

28. We | must locate

    he | will commit

29.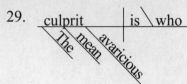
culprit | is \ who
The mean avaricious

30.
Mrs. Brite (investigator) | gave \ report
a clever
a thorough
(x)
on residences
the former
culprit's
police the
and me

LESSON 82 Demonstrative Pronouns

Practice 82

a. Blissful

b. Bliss

c. This painting

d. Those colors

e. This relative

f. These reasons

g. This key

Review Set 82

1. Culpable

2. curator

3. heroic

4. saltiness

5. proclamation

6. abstract

7. possessive

8. Whose

9. better

10. third, singular

11. Whom

12. We

13. Those

14. Since

15. a. angriest
    b. winning

16. complete sentence

17. To Alba, Dunn appears blissful.

18. a. adjective
    b. lav´ish
    c. Latin

19. Boise, the capital of Idaho, lies at the foot of the Rocky Mountains.

20. Your appointment with Dr. Gomez is on Mon., Jan. 2.

21. he

22. over the (hill)
    around the (rocks)

23. Lulu said, "Although I was born in Cheyenne, Wyoming, I now live in Salem, Oregon."

24. a. (is) stealing
    b. stole
    c. (has) stolen

25. My aunt read me a short story called "Adrift on an Ice Pan."

26. Fido stole my pencil, so I didn't do my homework.

27. Dear Mrs. Brite, P.I.,
    The culprit, I believe, was last seen in Juneau, Alaska.
    Respectfully,
    Officer Valiant

28. Badchek | fled | we | shall find

    we | are

29. culprit | swindled | whom
    The mean avaricious

30.

Officer Valiant (assistant) | sent | message

(with diagram lines showing: Mrs. Brite's, (x), me, a, about crimes, previous, Badchek's)

LESSON 83 Indefinite Pronouns

Practice 83

a. All; plural

b. Nobody; singular

c. are

d. are

e. is

f. has; its

g. wax, their

h. sells; it; is

i. subvert

j. subversion

More Practice 83

1. P
2. E
3. S
4. S
5. S
6. P
7. S
8. P
9. S
10. E
11. P
12. S
13. S
14. S
15. E
16. E
17. P
18. S
19. P
20. E

Review Set 83

1. Bliss
2. culprit
3. guide
4. Dauntless
5. similar
6. collective
7. nominative
8. theirs
9. fewer
10. third, singular
11. who
12. us
13. is
14. its
15. Wherever
16. plank
17. Looking up, Dana smiled.
18. grandchildren
19. The boll weevil, an insect with a long snout, ruined cotton crops in the South.
20. Both
21. subject
22. independent
23. Mrs. Brite, P.I., said, "Badchek cannot escape, for I have his name, address, and fingerprints."

24. a. (is) throwing
    b. threw
    c. (has) thrown

25. her

26. I. Fun at the ocean
    A. Fishing
    B. Surfing

27. Dear Mrs. Brite, P.I.,
    Obviously, Badchek does not live at 12 W. Palm Avenue, Juneau, Alaska. That place does not exist.
    Sincerely,
    Officer Valiant

28. canines | came   they | were

    plane | had left

29. Officer Valiant | should arrest | Whom
    the *intrepid*

30. Badchek (coward) | has written | checks
    a *culpable* (x) *nephew* *seven* *bad* *his*

LESSON 84   **Italics or Underline**

Practice 84

a. rapprochement

b. rapport

c. Time

d. is

e. Quercus

f. guapo

g. Betty Bee

More Practice 84 *See Master Worksheets*

Review Set 84

1. subvert

2. happy

3. blame

4. museum

5. kin

6. declarative

7. objective

8. Your

9. better

10. third, plural

11. whom

12. he

13. Is

14. Has, his or her

15. even though

16. What

17. Buenos días

18. palm

19. The island of Alcatraz, once a federal prison, lies in the middle of San Francisco Bay.

20. Neither

21. he

22. phrase

23. Officer Valiant replied, "Yes, as soon as we catch Badchek, we shall send him to Alcatraz."

24. a. (is) wearing
    b. wore
    c. (has) worn

25. B

26. No, I have not read a short story titled "Where the Sheep Went."

27. Dear Officer Valiant,
    On Friday, February 3, 2006, someone spotted Badchek in Columbus, Ohio.
                    Sincerely,
                    Mrs. Brite, P.I.

28.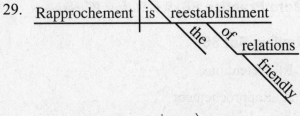

29.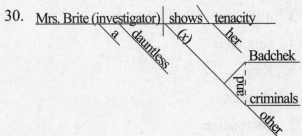

30.

LESSON 85   Irregular Verbs, Part 3

Practice 85

a. caught; (has) caught

b. came; (has) come

c. cost; (has) cost

d. dove or dived; (has) dived

e. dragged; (has) dragged

f. drew; (has) drawn

g. drowned; (has) drowned

h. drove; (has) driven

i. eaten

j. found

k. drove

l. cost

m. forgave

n. caught

o. flew

p. fell

q. grandiloquent

r. pretentious

More Practice 85 *See Master Worksheets*

Review Set 85

1. Rapport

2. Subversion

3. happiness

4. guilty

5. Akin

6. plural

7. possessive

8. hers

9. best

10. third, plural

11. who

12. us

13. come

14. have, their

15. Until

16. Whose

17. Kim

18. houseflies

19. The Gila monster, Arizona's biggest lizard, is the only poisonous lizard in the United States.

20. compound sentence

21. subject

22. in California's Humboldt Bay by H.D. Bendixsen

23. Mrs. Brite, P.I., said, "We have not caught him, but we shall before summer."

24. a. (is) forgiving
    b. forgave
    c. (has) forgiven

25. me

26. Yes, I know the song "I've Been Working on the Railroad."

27. My dear Ms. Hoo,
    Get plenty of rest, exercise, and fresh air.
    Warm regards,
    Katy Diddit, R.N.

28.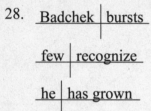

29.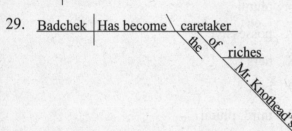

30.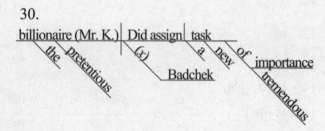

LESSON 86   Irregular Verbs, Part 4

Practice 86

a. hid; (has) hidden or hid

b. held; (has) held

c. laid; (has) laid

d. led; (has) led

e. lent; (has) lent

f. mistook; (has) mistaken

g. put; (has) put

h. sold; (has) sold

i. hid

j. held

k. laid

l. led

m. colossal

n. colossus

More Practice 86 *See Master Worksheets*

Review Set 86

1. Pretentious
2. Rapprochement
3. different
4. happiness
5. Kin
6. abstract
7. nominative
8. Whose
9. fewer
10. first, plural
11. Whom
12. I
13. gone
14. has, his or her
15. as if, that
16. optimistic
17. Seafoam Joy
18. a. noun
    b. mīm
    c. Greek
19. Nashville, the capital of Tennessee, is famous for country music.
20. a. messiest
    b. thinner

21. they

22. phrase

23. Mrs. Brite, P.I., said, "Although a deceptive, malicious witness has given me false reports, I shall still find the culprit."

24. a. (is) driving
    b. drove
    c. (has) driven

25. me

26. In my opinion, the short story should be titled "Badchek on the Loose."

27. My dear Mrs. Hoo,
    You may see Dr. Rivas on Monday, February 6.
    Warm regards,
    Katy Diddit, R.N.

28. Jake | has ridden   he | is

    he | must milk

29. speech | Was \ joke

    Mr. Knothead's grandiloquent   a

30. Mr. K. (billionaire) | Has given | key

    the foolish (x)   a to safe

    Badchek   the

LESSON 87   Irregular Verbs, Part 5

Practice 87

a. took; (has) taken

b. set; (has) set

c. taught; (has) taught

d. told; (has) told

e. woke; (has) woken

f. sprang or sprung; (has) sprung

g. strove; (has) striven

h. shut; (has) shut

i. written

j. slept

k. thought

l. taught

m. told

n. woken

o. sat

p. shut

q. coerce

r. coercion

More Practice 87 *See Master Worksheets*

Review Set 87

1. colossus

2. pretentious

3. understanding

4. Avaricious

5. destruction

6. compound

7. objective

8. theirs

9. better

10. first, singular

11. whom

12. we

13. lay, slept

14. has, his or her

15. as, if

16. complete sentence

17. After the show, time stood still.

18. dropperfuls

19. South Dakota, the Mount Rushmore State, has a large area of forest called the Black Hills.

20. Bozo

21. object

22. Across the (field)
    under the (fence)
    over the (hill)

23. Katy Diddit, R.N., said, "I wrote to Ms. Hoo, but she has not written back."

24. a. (is) bringing
    b. brought
    c. (has) brought

25. B

26. That song, I believe, is called "Over the Waves."

27. Dear Grandmother,
       I have striven to do my best. Thank you for helping me.
                      Love,
                      Benito

28.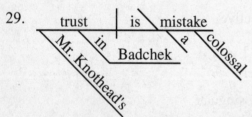

29.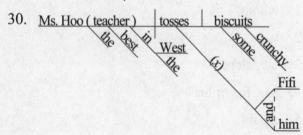

30. Ms. Hoo (teacher) tosses biscuits ...

LESSON 88   The Exclamation Mark • The Question Mark

Practice 88

a. Wow! That … spectacular!

b. Do you understand Greek?

c. Who painted *Blue Boy*?

d. I know! It's Thomas Gainsborough!

e. complacency

f. complacent

Review Set 88

1. coerce
2. large
3. showy
4. reestablishment
5. greedy
6. imperative
7. objective
8. Who
9. better
10. third, singular
11. whom
12. she
13. taken, hung
14. have, their
15. While, so that
16. luminous
17. complacent
18. weigh
19. Dagny, a complacent player, seems unmotivated now.
20. compound sentence
21. she

22. phrase

23. Chloe asked, "Have you heard from Ms. Hoo, Katy?"

24. a. (is) buying
    b. bought
    c. (has) bought

25. me

26. What a silly story! It should be titled "Mr. Knothead's Colossal Mistake."

27. Dear Benito,
    Have you seen my old shoes? They are made out of string, straw, and wood.
    Love,
    Grandpa

28. Butch | has been growling

    Fifi | has been cowering

    Bozo | will save

29. Mr. Knothead | Has been \ imprudent

30.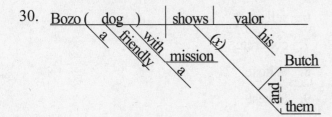

LESSON 89   Subject-Verb Agreement, Part 1

Practice 89

a. was

b. were

c. raise

d. makes

e. make

f. has

g. languid

h. languish

More Practice 89

1. sound

2. are

3. swim

4. are

5. has

6. were

7. have

8. sees

Review Set 89

1. Complacent

2. Coercion

3. large

4. reestablishment

5. Avarice

6. possessive

7. possessive

8. Their, yours

9. fewer

10. third, singular

11. who

12. us

13. kept, slain

14. has, his or her

15. likes

16. linguist

17. Pool of Waterlilies

18. paint brushes

19. Tina, Butch's owner, spends three hours a day training her dog.

20. a. worrisome
    b. funnier

21. object

22. independent

23. Leo shouted, "Help! Since you are taller than I, can you reach that apple?"

24. a. (is) drawing
    b. drew
    c. (has) drawn

25. him

26. That song, I think, is called "Little Bunny Fufu."

27. Dear Tina,
    Why is your dog so crabby? Have you taught him no manners?
    With concern,
    Cousin Juan

28. Although, until

29.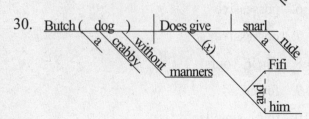

30.

LESSON 90   Subject-Verb Agreement, Part 2

Practice 90

a. pictures | were   were

b. stations | were   were

c. kinds | are   are

d. leader | goes   goes

e. trucks | come   come

---

f. noxious

g. innocuous

More Practice 90

1. sits
2. weighs
3. is
4. go
5. are
6. breaks
7. makes
8. looks

Review Set 90

1. languish
2. contentment
3. force
4. large
5. burden
6. sells
7. concrete
8. Whose
9. fewest
10. first, plural
11. whom
12. they
13. risen, woken
14. has, its
15. like
16. sentence fragment
17. With this, Olga can repair the chair.
18. a. noun
    b. dī′ kast
    c. Greek
19. Frankfort, the capital of Kentucky, lies along the Kentucky River.

20. biscuits

21. she

22. During the (night)
    toward my (muffins)

23. Lucy cries, "Watch out! A branch has broken, and it might fall on you."

24. a. (is) beating
    b. beat
    c. (has) beaten

25. her

26. As I remember, Ms. Hoo wrote an article titled "My Students' Lovable Pets."

27. Dear Juan,
      I have only had Butch for two months, three days, one hour, and five minutes. Please be patient with me.
                   Your cousin,
                   Tina

28. Though, wherever

29.

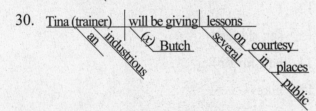

30.

LESSON 91   Subject-Verb Agreement, Part 3

Practice 91

a. aren't

b. is

c. weren't

d. There are

e. has

f. obfuscation

g. obfuscate

More Practice 91

1. is
2. is
3. needs
4. wants
5. is
6. knows
7. has
8. understands
9. There are
10. There's
11. isn't
12. doesn't
13. don't
14. aren't
15. aren't

Review Set 91

1. Innocuous
2. Languid
3. content
4. force
5. encumbrance
6. were
7. collective
8. your
9. friendlier
10. second
11. Who
12. us
13. led, swam
14. have, their
15. knows

16. There are

17. <u>Skeedaddle</u>

18. freight

19. Mount Whitney, California's tallest mountain, has more climbers than any other peak in the Sierra Nevada.

20. simple sentence

21. subject

22. dependent

23. Harold yells, "Don't go! Before you leave, I must warn you about the dangers."

24. a. (is) falling
    b. fell
    c. (has) fallen

25. A

26. I. Aesop's fables
    A. "The Tortoise and the Hare"
    B. "The Lion and the Mouse"
    C. "The Cat and the Bell"

27. Dear Tina,
    Please come to our family reunion in Jefferson City, Missouri, on Tuesday, January 2, 2007.
    Your cousin,
    Juan

28. As soon as, unless

29.

retirement | Will be <

restful

and

serene

Ms. Hoo's

30.

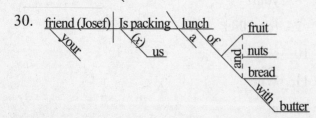
friend (Josef) | Is packing | lunch

your

(x) us

a

of

fruit

and

nuts

bread

with

butter

LESSON 92 **Subject-Verb Agreement, Part 4**

Practice 92

a. covers

b. is

c. has

d. was

e. concise

f. conciseness

Review Set 92

1. obfuscate

2. antonyms

3. weak

4. satisfaction

5. exalt

6. come

7. exclamatory

8. whom

9. many

10. possessive

11. who

12. I

13. sat, ridden

14. has, his or her

15. hike

16. has

17. <u>Pytilia melba</u>

18. finches

19. The melba finch, an aggressive bird, eats seeds and insects.

20. a. penniless
    b. truly

21. he

22. phrase

23. "May I please have more broccoli?" asked Mateo.

24. a. (is) finding
    b. found
    c. (has) found

25. me

26. Dad said, "I'm sorry, Luz, the broccoli is all gone."

27. Dear Juan,
    May I bring Butch? He is my friend, companion, and guard dog.
                    Your cousin,
                    Tina

28. After, because

29.

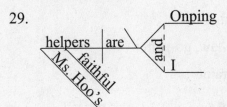

30.

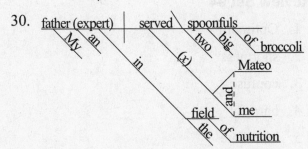

LESSON 93   Negatives • Double Negatives

Practice 93

a. had

b. could

c. anything

d. ever

e. ever

f. minimum

g. optimum

More Practice 93

1. any, any

2. any

3. anybody

4. either

5. anyone

6. anywhere

7. any

8. ever

9. any

10. anything

Review Set 93

1. concise

2. unclear

3. harmless

4. energy

5. synonyms

6. go

7. possessive

8. can

9. bigger

10. first, singular

11. Who, hers

12. us

13. made, shaken

14. hasn't, her

15. plants

16. There are

17. For sewing, machines are helpful.

18. queens of Spain

19. The people of Olympia, the capital of Washington, are called "Olympians."

20. compound

21. subject

22. Aboard (ship)
    along the (coastline)
    amid a (pod)
    of (whales)

23. "That broccoli tastes delicious!" exclaims Mateo.

24. a. (is) building
    b. built
    c. (has) built

25. her

26. Luz said, "Please cook more broccoli, Dad."

27. Dear Tina,
      There is a dog hotel at 43 State Street, Jefferson City, Missouri.
                        Your cousin,
                        Juan

28. Whenever, where

29.
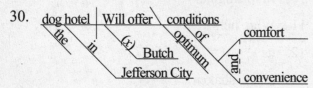

30.
dog hotel | Will offer \ conditions
the \ in \ (a) Butch \ of \ optimum \ comfort
Jefferson City \ and \ convenience

LESSON 94   The Hyphen: Compound Nouns and Numbers

Practice 94

a. ostracize

b. ostracism

c. know-how

d. write-up

e. twenty-five

f. 13-20

More Practice 94

1. twenty-five

2. forty-seven

3. seventy-six

4. ninety-eight

5. twenty-first

6. thirty-second

7. forty-fifth

8. eighty-third

9. self-confidence

10. work-out

11. sister-in-law, go-getter

12. self-restraint

Review Set 94

1. Optimum

2. shortness

3. confuse

4. harmful

5. humiliate

6. sits

7. abstract

8. any

9. biggest

10. objective

11. Theirs, yours

12. I

13. woven, sold

14. haven't, their

15. wakes

16. was

17. patch

18. a. adjective
    b. di luks´
    c. French (going back to Latin)

19. Forty-two people attended the get-together.

20. ostrich

21. they

22. phrase

23. "If Butch howls, will you quiet him?" asked Tina.

24. a. (is) catching
    b. caught
    c. (has) caught

25. A

26. I shall title my essay "The Smooth, Enjoyable Voyage."

27. My dear cousin,
    Butch will stay with me, for he requires a soft bed, healthful food, and lots of attention.
                                    Love,
                                    Tina

28. than, when

29.

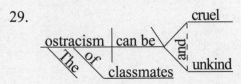

30.

LESSON 95   Adverbs that Tell "How"

Practice 95

a. "proudly" modifies "sits"

b. "rapidly" modifies "burn"

c. "quickly" and "easily" modify "repaired"

d. adjective; modifies "lecture"

e. adverb; modifies "Did speak"

f. adjective; modifies "turn"

g. adverb; modifies "turned"

h. paltriness

i. Paltry

Review Set 95

1. ostracize

2. least

3. concise

4. confusion

5. antonyms

6. is

7. compound

8. any

9. fewer

10. first, plural

11. Whom

12. us

13. mistook, thought

14. haven't, their

15. wake

16. was

17. David

18. can openers

19. For exercise, we did seventy-five sit-ups.

20. compound

21. him

22. independent

23. Juan said, "I rented a large room for the party, but only a few people are coming."

24. a. (is) eating
    b. ate
    c. (has) eaten

25. skillfully modifies "write"

26. The scariest chapter was titled "Lost in the Jungle."

27. The colors of the rainbow, as I recall, are red, orange, yellow, green, blue, indigo, and violet.

28. as though, since

29.

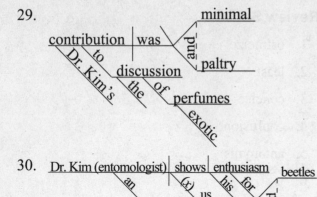

30.

LESSON 96   Using the Adverb *Well*

Practice 96

a. well

b. good

c. well

d. good

e. well

f. perjure

g. Perjury

More Practice 96

1. well

2. well

3. well

4. good

5. good

6. good

7. well

8. good

9. well

10. good

Review Set 96

1. Paltry

2. ostracize

3. best

4. antonyms

5. true

6. are

7. well

8. has

9. tiredest

10. nominative

11. ours, theirs

12. he

13. lent, wrote

14. has, his

15. feeds

16. boards

17. <u>Alice in Wonderland</u>

18. lilac bushes

19. Thirty-three show-offs were trying to get attention.

20. bicycle

21. object

22. clause

23. My aunt asked if I would like any lemons, oranges, or avocados from her trees.

24. a. (is) biting
    b. bit
    c. (has) bitten

25. blissfully modifies "slept"

26. Jason wrote a poem and titled it "If I Were an Ant."

27. Please remember, I have moved to 960 Fox Lane, Frazzle Park, Oregon.

28. Before, so that, where

29. testimony | must have been \ perjury
   Badchek's / outrageous / in court

30.
Dr. Axle (herpetologist) | provided | information
   a / (x) / valuable / about — reptiles
   and
   Lily — amphibians
   and
   me

LESSON 97 The Hyphen: Compound Adjectives

Practice 97

a. A-frame

b. none

c. re-cover

d. eight-ounce

e. Mud-coated

f. Plagiarism

g. plagiarize

Review Set 97

1. Perjury

2. Paltriness

3. exclude

4. lowest

5. Dogmatic

6. costs

7. well

8. any

9. fewer

10. first, plural

11. Who's

12. us

13. given, taught

14. has, his or her

15. sings

16. are

17. A Thatched Cottage by a Tree

18. a. verb
    b. en trap´
    c. French

19. I spent forty-five minutes scrubbing my paint-stained shirt.

20. simple

21. she

22. independent clause

23. Meg asks, "Would you like any lemons, oranges, or avocados?"

24. a. (is) feeling
    b. felt
    c. (has) felt

25. concisely modifies "writes"

26. An interesting article as titled "The Return of the Lynx."

27. Herbert, my oldest brother, graduated on June 16, 2006.

28. Even though, that

29. school | was \ hike
   Mother's / elementary / a / four-mile / from — home / her

30.
Arachnologist (M. H.) | showed | collection
   (x) / her / large / of — spiders
   and
   Dan — scorpions
   and
   them

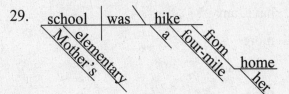

LESSON 98   Adverbs that Tell "Where"

Practice 98

a. anywhere; can nap

b. home; have come

c. out; might have gone

d. around; wanders

e.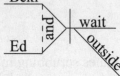

f.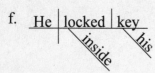

g. profusion

h. profuse

Review Set 98

1. plagiarize
2. lie
3. insignificant
4. excluding
5. Concrete
6. wears
7. good
8. have, any
9. more
10. possessive
11. their
12. they
13. lost, stood
14. There are
15. sing
16. are

17. were, where
18. car parts
19. James hammered twenty-four nails into two-by-four lumber.
20. a. jogging
    b. tried
21. subject
22. phrase
23. "I patted the goat's head, and it took a bite of my sleeve!" exclaimed Rondo.
24. a. (is) flying
    b. flew
    c. (has) flown
25. suddenly modifies "leap" (tells "how")
    up modifies "leap" (tells "where")
26. Riding home from Denver, Colorado, my sister sang "Old MacDonald Had a Farm" over and over again.
27. One the other hand, you could paint the table red, white, or blue.
28. Because, even though
29. bottle | Does look \ empty
    that / two-liter / of / water
30. Arachnologist (Mari Hunt) | lifted | specimen
    carefully / up / each

LESSON 99   Word Division

Practice 99

a. no division

b. can- did

c. choco- late

d. no division

e. no division

f. forty- seven

g. prologue

h. epilogue

More Practice 99

1. no division

2. bliss- ful

3. anti- dote

4. no division

5. con- ceal

6. super- sonic

7. no division

8. con- trite

9. la- goon

10. no division

11. no division

12. pal- try

13. ig- nite

14. per- jure

15. pre- pare

16. no division

17. pad- dle

18. no division

19. hemi- sphere

20. pro- logue

Review Set 99

1. Profuse

2. Plagiarism

3. lying

4. little

5. Intangible

6. were

7. well

8. hasn't, any

9. most

10. third, plural

11. Whose

12. we

13. swung, run

14. there are

15. are

16. were

17. The White Horse

18. handfuls

19. Watching the penguin's egg hatch was a once-in-a-lifetime experience.

20. a. no division
    b. epi- logue

21. her

22. dependent clause

23. "Ms. Hoo, do goats normally eat sweaters?" asked Rondo.

24. a. (is) costing
    b. cost
    c. (has) cost

25. gladly modifies "sits" (tells "how")
    nearby modifies "sits" (tells "where")

26. I read an article titled "Russia's Giant Bears."

27. Lee B. Guo, R.N., has moved to 940 Fast Lane, Atlanta, Georgia.

28. When, if

29.

```
Celly (horse) | Does look \ healthy
   the \ twenty-year-old
```

30.

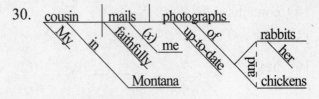

LESSON 100 — Adverbs that Tell "When"

Practice 100

a. Tonight; will build

b. later; can fish

c. ever; Have seen

d. yesterday; read

e.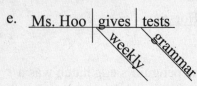
Ms. Hoo | gives | tests
weekly / grammar

f.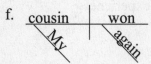
cousin | won
My / again

g. impropriety

h. propriety

Review Set 100

1. prologue

2. abundance

3. ideas

4. perjure

5. knowledge

6. was

7. well

8. has, any

9. fewer

10. objective

11. Your, ours

12. we

13. held, shut

14. contains

15. has

16. has

17. The Forbidden Door

18. pocket knives

19. Julio has completed fifty-four life-sized drawings.

20. a. no division
    b. un- feigned

21. he

22. clause

23. "Rondo, you have a hole in your shirt!" exclaims Ms. Hoo.

24. a. (is) fighting
    b. fought
    c. (has) fought

25. quickly modifies "tiptoes" (tells "how") out modifies "tiptoes" (tells "where")

26. Carl Sandburg wrote the poem "Buffalo Dusk."

27. This library book was due Friday, February 3, 2006, I believe.

28. never, again

29. Celly (stallion) | Has grown \ tamer
    your / twenty-year-old

30.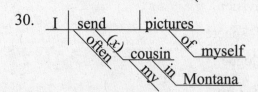
I | send | pictures
often (x) cousin of myself
my in Montana

LESSON 101 — Adverbs that Tell "How Much"

Practice 101

a. incredibly; talented

b. almost; missed

c. too; fast

d. n't; could understand

e. terribly; grumpy

f. enigma

g. enigmatic

h.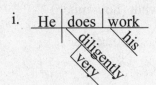

i.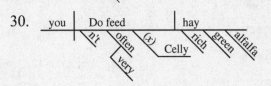

More Practice 101 *See Master Worksheets*

Review Set 101

1. Propriety

2. end

3. abundant

4. theft

5. Cognizant

6. were

7. good

8. is, any

9. fewest

10. first, plural

11. Whose

12. us

13. told, hid

14. pounces

15. has

16. has

17. For Amparo, Marco will do his best.

18. chiefs of staff

19. Forty-two English-speaking scientists have come from Japan.

20. a. no division
    b. silver- ware

21. him

22. independent clause

23. "Students," asks Ms. Hoo, "have you studied well?"

24. a. (is) forgetting
    b. forgot
    c. (has) forgotten

25. timidly modifies "glances" (tells "how")
    around modifies "glances" (tells "where")

26. The last chapter, "How They Caught the Culprit," is my favorite.

27. Yes, Neil B. Smart, Ph.D., teaches chemistry, physics, and Russian.

28. terribly (how much), late (when)

29.

30.

LESSON 102   Comparison Adverbs

Practice 102

a. more ferociously

b. most quickly

c. better

d. farthest

e. worse, worst

f. candid

g. candor

More Practice 102

1. better

2. best

3. farther

4. less

5. least

6. slower

7. longer

8. harder

Review Set 102

1. enigma

2. improper

3. introduction

4. profusion

5. aware

6. was

7. well

8. aren't, any

9. longest

10. objective

11. Who's

12. we

13. gotten, shined

14. are

15. have

16. was

17. <u>Enigma, Enigmatic</u>

18. flu viruses

19. A color-blind painter used twenty-one different colors on the kitchen walls.

20. a. can- dor
    b. no division

21. he

22. phrase

23. "Catch those thieves!" cries Officer Valiant.

24. a. (is) fleeing
    b. fled
    c. (has) fled

25. fearlessly modifies "moves" (tells "how") ahead modifies "moves" (tells "where")

26. Omar titled his essay "Out of the Darkness."

27. Our essays are due, I believe, on Monday, February 26.

28. now (when), somewhat (how much)

29.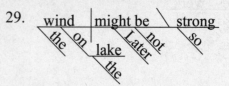

30.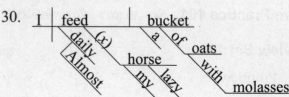

LESSON 103   The Semicolon

Practice 103

a. …blue, blew; hear, here; and no, know

b. …spring;

c. …home;

d. monarchy

e. anarchy

More Practice 103 *See Master Worksheets*

Review Set 103

1. Candor

2. Enigmatic

3. conformity

4. epilogue

5. Extravagant

6. come

7. good

8. has, any

9. longer

10. nominative

11. Your, ours

12. I

13. sprung, hanged

14. is

15. recycle

16. has

17. <u>Good Hope</u>

18. I remembered all the states and their capitals except for Madison, Wisconsin; Pierre, South Dakota; and Topeka, Kansas.

19. Their one-time offer was less desirable than a hand-me-down toothbrush.

20. a. dis- close
    b. no division

21. me

22. dependent clause

23. "Have you caught Badchek?" asked Ms. Hoo.

24. a. (is) bursting
    b. burst
    c. (has) burst

25. profusely modifies "grow" (tells "how") here modifies "grow" (tells "where")

26. Howard R. Garis, a newspaperman, wrote the short story "Uncle Wiggily and the Big Rat."

27. The culprits, it seems, are Badchek, Whipper, and Shadow.

28. Sometimes (when), too (how much)

29.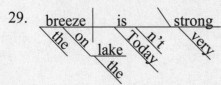

30.
H. R. G. | would write | stories

LESSON 104   Adverb Usage

Practice 104

a. parsimonious

b. parsimony

c. surely

d. really

e. really

f. badly

g. badly

More Practice 104

1. surely

2. certainly

3. really

4. really

5. really

6. badly

7. bad

8. badly

Review Set 104

1. Anarchy

2. honest

3. mystery

4. impropriety

5. antonyms

6. was, really

7. certainly, well

8. isn't, anybody

9. more

10. first, plural

11. Whom

12. We

13. wrung, hung

14. hears

15. recycles

16. is

17. <u>Frazzle Express</u>

18. He remembers her face; however, her name escapes him.

19. Mother has a curly, wash-and-wear hairdo.

20. a. tun- dra
    b. no division

21. she

22. clause

23. "There's smoke!" shouts Michael.

24. a. (is) diving
    b. dove or dived
    c. (has) dived

25. intuitively modifies "knew" (tells "how") there modifies "was" (tells "where")

26. Conrad, a camp counselor, played the guitar and sang "Kookaburra."

27. As we sat around the campfire, Conrad told us a long, scary story.

28. Afterward (when), terribly (how much)

29.

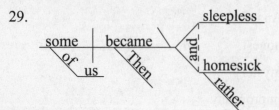

30.

C. (counselor) did tell story

LESSON 105 — The Colon

Practice 105

a. 6:00 a.m.

b. I am taking the following classes: English, math, history, science, and P.E.

c. Dear Madam:
   Please send me your special recipe for the pea soup…

d. Abraham Lincoln spoke these words: "Most folks are about as happy as they make up their minds to be."

e. desecrate

f. consecrate

Review Set 105

1. Parsimony

2. ruler

3. honesty

4. mysterious

5. synonyms

6. itches, badly

7. surely, well

8. isn't, anything

9. most

10. possessive

11. Who

12. us

13. bought

14. hear

15. race

16. is

17. <u>The Japanese Bridge</u>

18. Rain fell; it beat on our tents.

19. All twenty-three campers wore water-repellent ponchos.

20. a. con- trite
    b. no division

21. me

22. Dear Teachers:
    By 2:00 p.m., I must have the following: your roll sheets, your grades, and your seating charts.
    Respectfully,
    Mr. Stoneman

23. Dr. Kim asks, "Is there a fire?"

24. Yes, she was born on Monday, May 10, 1948.

25. generously modifies "passes" (tells "how") around modifies "passes" (tells "where")

26. Erik, a young camper, prefers stories such as "Uncle Wiggily and the Watermelon."

27. If Conrad tells another dark, mysterious story, we shall turn on big, bright flashlights.

28. dreadfully (how much), later (when)

29.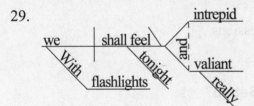

30.

LESSON 106

The Prepositional Phrase as an Adverb • Diagramming

Practice 106

a. from hard work; come

b. in the city; lives

c. of prepositions; weary

d. for another lesson; ready

e. concerning grammar; wise

f.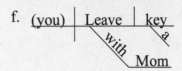

g.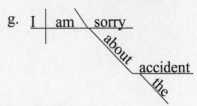

h. beguile

i. guile

More Practice 106

1.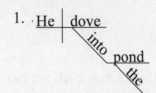

2.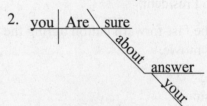

3.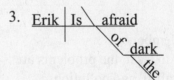

4.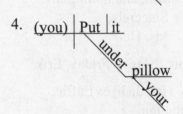

5.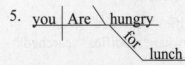

Review Set 106

1. consecrate

2. stingy

3. government

4. honest

5. father's

6. really, itch

7. certainly, badly

8. anything

9. farther

10. first, plural

11. Who's

12. we

13. saw

14. exercises

15. sweeps

16. is

17. <u>Tribune</u>

18. We saw the White House; however, we did not see the President.

19. I pushed the fast-forward button during the three-hour movie.

20. a. be- guile
    b. no division

21. she

22. Dear Council Members:
    From greatest to least, the problems are these: traffic, graffiti, and pollution.
    Sincerely,
    Ms. Hoo

23. Conrad exclaims, "Happy Friday, Erik!"

24. Obviously, Ms. Hoo dislikes traffic, graffiti, and pollution.

25. carefully modifies "searched" (tells "how"); everywhere modifies "searched" (tells "where")

26. Luz, a guitarist, ended with the song "Make New Friends."

27. While Conrad sleeps, Erik plans a clever, harmless prank.

28. Tomorrow (when); very (how much)

29.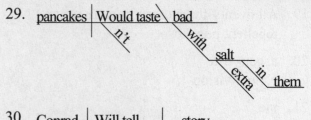

30. Conrad | Will tell | story

LESSON 107   Preposition or Adverb? • Preposition Usage

Practice 107

a. adverb

b. preposition

c. preposition

d. adverb

e. into

f. Between

g. besides

h. digressions

i. digress

Review Set 107

1. Guile

2. desecrate

3. stinginess

4. Monarchy

5. mother's

6. go, really

7. surely, well

8. any

9. farthest

10. into, among

11. Yours, theirs

12. us

13. seen

14. have

15. sweep

16. fits

17. <u>adios</u>

18. The bus will stop in Phoenix, Arizona; Santa Fe, New Mexico; and Oklahoma City, Oklahoma.

19. Twenty-eight singers performed a one-of-a-kind concert.

20. a. ar- dent
    b. no division

21. her

22. Dear Counselors:
    Please close the cabins as follows: sweep floors, take out trash, and lock doors.
    Sincerely,
    Mr. Vasquez

23. "Have Badchek and she fled to another country?" asked Ms. Hoo.

24. They have fled, I believe, to Ottawa, Canada.

25. adverb

26. I especially liked the last chapter, "A Warm Wind."

27. As the moon casts shadows, Erik imagines big, hungry beasts outside the tent.

28. Later (when); thoroughly (how much)

29.

30.

Practice 108

a. futility

b. futile

c. sisters-in-law's

d. Rob's

e. kittens'

f. friends'

g. child's

h. bus's

More Practice 108

1. isthmus's

2. tributary's

3. delta's

4. estuary's

5. meteor's

6. kin's

7. story's

8. culprit's

9. deer's

10. days'

11. miners'

12. fish's

13. girls'

14. sheep's

15. stories'

16. men's

Review Set 108

1. digress

2. mislead

3. sacred

4. money

5. mother

6. writes, really

7. surely, well

8. was

9. cleaner

10. beside

11. Whose

12. We

13. saw

14. have

15. sweep

16. fits

17. <u>Waverly Bliss</u>

18. I remember Phoenix; however, I must have slept through our stop in Santa Fe.

19. From the third-story window, she could see moss-covered rocks.

20. a. fu- tile
    b. no division

21. she

22. Dear Mr. Vasquez:

    My cabin needs the following: paint, light bulbs, carpet.

    Sincerely,
    Conrad Dudd

23. Conrad shouts, "Look at that tarantula!"

24. a. boss's
    b. Chris's
    c. horses'

25. preposition

26. Erik will title his essay "A Long Week at Camp Woisme."

27. When Erik grows up, he might become a kind, thoughtful camp counselor.

28. Then (when); almost (how much)

29.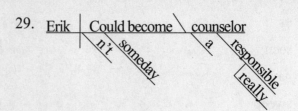

30.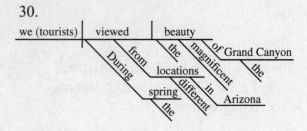

LESSON 109 — The Apostrophe: Contractions, Omitting Digits and Letters

Practice 109

a. haven't

b. I've, workin'

c. '48, '02

d. shouldn't

e. they'd

f. dissent

g. dissension

More Practice 109 *See Master Worksheets*

Review Set 109

1. Futile

2. digression

3. deceit

4. destroy

5. Imprudent

6. writes, really

7. really badly

8. is

9. cleanest

10. besides

11. Who

12. I ("swim" omitted)

13. saw

14. has

15. You're

16. cuts well

17. <u>Charlotte's Web</u>

18. I am tired; nevertheless, I shall clean my room.

19. You can buy a five-pound melon for ninety-nine cents.

20. a. no division
    b. be- guile

21. a. wouldn't
    b. they're

22. Dear Sir or Madam:
       Why does my morning newspaper never arrive until 2:00 p.m. or later?
                        Your customer,
                        Ms. Hoo

23. Erik asked, "Have you seen my flashlight?"

24. a. artists'
    b. Melody's
    c. lady's

25. preposition

26. Melody, my niece, sang "Oklahoma."

27. If she sings it again, her sleepy, irritable friends might complain.

28. Tonight (when); terribly (how much)

29.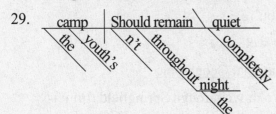

30.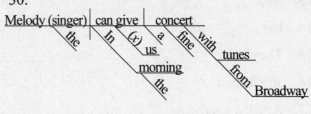

LESSON 110   The Complex Sentence • The Compound-Complex Sentence

Practice 110

  a. simple

  b. compound-complex

  c. complex

  d. compound

  e. apathetic

  f. apathy

More Practice 110

1. complex

2. compound

3. simple

4. compound-complex

Review Set 110

1. dissent

2. hopelessness

3. subject

4. beguile

5. wise

6. goes, really

7. surely, well

8. anybody

9. more

10. into

11. Who's

12. he ("is" omitted)

13. seen

14. has

15. They're

16. smells bad

17. <u>Apathy</u>, <u>apathetic</u>

18. My room is messy; therefore, I shall clean it.

19. My twenty-year-old sister took a five-day vacation in Arizona.

20. a. no division
    b. air- plane

21. a. you're
    b. can't

22. Dear Sir or Madam:
    I wish to cancel my subscription to the newspaper.
    A dissatisfied customer,
    Ms. Hoo

23. At Thursday's track meet, Grandpa yelled, "Run Amelia!"

24. a. actors'
    b. Andy's
    c. James's

25. adverb

26. Kurt wrote the poem "If I Were You."

27. compound-complex

28. Soon (when); vastly (how much)

29.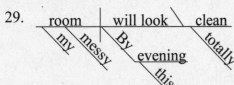

30.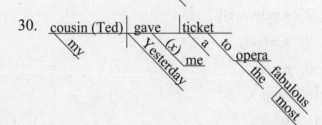

LESSON 111   Active or Passive Voice

Practice 111

a. passive

b. active

c. passive

d. active

e. elucidate

f. lucid

Review Set 111

1. Apathy

2. disagreement

3. hopeless

4. digression

5. imprudent

6. leads, really

7. surely, well

8. a

9. most

10. onto

11. Whose

12. I ("am" omitted)

13. saw

14. have

15. You're

16. fit well

17. <u>National Geographic</u>

18. We drove through Springfield, Illinois; Indianapolis, Indiana; and Columbus, Ohio.

19. My sister-in-law borrowed a six-foot ladder.

20. a. con- cise
    b. no division

21. a. they'll
    b. haven't

22. Please excuse the following students: Amy Ngo, Rod Perez, and Rosa Green.

23. "Are you from Georgia?" asked Mark.

24. a. states'
    b. Amy's
    c. Avis's

25. adverb

26. Her second song was "Consider Yourself."

27. complex sentence

28. Later (when); more (how much)

29.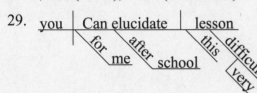

30.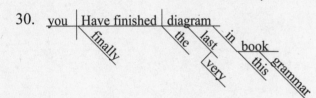

LESSON 112   Interjections

Practice 112

a. Whoops

b. Hey

c. Bam

d. Yuck

e. Hurrah | That | is \ news
                        \ good

f. Shh | people | are thinking

g. finale

h. finalize

Review Set 112

1. last

2. concern

3. finalize

4. clear

5. elucidate

6. has, really

7. surely, well

8. a

9. more

10. onto

11. Whose

12. I ("am" omitted)

13. saw

14. have

15. Your

16. cuts well

17. passive voice

18. This bus passes through Denver, Colorado; Cheyenne, Wyoming; and Helena, Montana.

19. My brother-in-law has an eight-foot python.

20. a. be- guile
    b. no division

21. a. you're
    b. they're

22. Please call the following people: James Lu, John Garcia, and Rachel Cohen.

23. "Have you caught any fish?" asked Daisy.

24. a. countries'
    b. Kerry's
    c. Mr. Davis's

25. preposition

26. For the grand finale, the band played "America the Beautiful."

27. compound sentence

28. Then (when); most (how much)

29.

```
we | shall finalize | plan
  \              \
   \Tomorrow      \our   \for improvement
                         \the  \of school
                                    \our
```

30.

```
Ah   we | have finished | diagram
      \                   \
       \finally   \the  \last  \in   book
                        \very       \this  \grammar
```

Circle the correct word(s) to complete sentences 1–5.

1. A (subject, (sentence)) is a word group that expresses a complete thought.
(1)

2. The two essential parts of a sentence are the subject and the (predator, (predicate)).
(1)

3. The ((subject), predicate) tells whom or what the sentence is about.
(1)

4. The (subject, (predicate)) tells what the subject does, is, or is like.
(1)

5. A complete sentence has ((two), four) main parts.
(1)

6. For a–e, circle the correct definition. (1 point for each correct answer)

     (a) Essential means (opposite, (necessary), unnecessary).
     (1)

     (b) Antonyms are (dinosaurs, (opposites), optimists).
     (2)

     (c) Abundant means (scarce, (plentiful), essential).
     (3)

     (d) Pessimism is the belief that things are going to get (better, (worse)).
     (4)

     (e) *Their* and *there* are (synonyms, antonyms, (homophones)).
     (5)

For 7–10, write whether the sentence is declarative, interrogative, exclamatory, or imperative.

7. Rosa Parks refused to give up her seat in a bus. _____declarative_____
(2)

8. How cold does it get in Alaska? _____interrogative_____
(2)

9. Bring water on your hike through the desert. _____imperative_____
(2)

10. It's a rattlesnake! _____exclamatory_____
(2)

Circle the simple subject of sentences 11–13.

11. Some (people) in Arkansas listen to delightful kitchen bands.
(3)

12. Can (Jenny) play the fiddle?
(3)

13. (Archaeologists) have found dinosaur fossils in Colorado.
(3)

Circle the simple predicate of sentences 14–16.

14. Some people in Arkansas (listen) to delightful kitchen bands.
(4)

15. Jenny (can play) the fiddle.
(4)

16. Archaeologists (have found) dinosaur fossils in Colorado.
(4)

For 17–19, write whether the word group is a sentence fragment or a complete sentence.

17. Picking seeds from the watermelon. _sentence fragment_
(5)

18. Mount McKinley is the tallest mountain in North America. _complete sentence_
(5)

19. To catch a catfish in the pond. _sentence fragment_
(5)

20. Draw a vertical line between the subject and predicate parts of the sentence below.
(1)

Horseshoe crabs | have endured the changes of man.

Circle the correct word(s) to complete sentences 1–5.

1. Yesterday Martin (fry, fries, (fried)) catfish for supper.
(10)

2. An alligator (sleep, (sleeps)) in the Everglades.
(9)

3. Leon (ski, (skis)) in Vail, Colorado.
(9)

4. The sentence below is (declarative, interrogative, (exclamatory), imperative).
(2)

   Look at all the ladybugs!

5. The sentence below is (declarative, interrogative, exclamatory, (imperative)).
(2)

   Use sunscreen at the beach.

6. For a–e, circle the correct definition. (1 point for each correct answer)

   (a) ((Its), It's) is the possessive form of *it*.
   (6)

   (b) To disclose is to (hide, (uncover), sneeze).
   (7)

   (c) ((Geology), Archipelago, Flora) is earth science.
   (8)

   (d) An archipelago is a chain of many (beads, (islands), events).
   (9)

   (e) Fauna is (plant, (animal)) life.
   (10)

7. On the lines below, make a complete sentence from the following sentence fragment:
(6)

   After finishing this test, _example: I shall relax and read a good book. (Answers will vary.)_

   _____

Circle the action verb in sentences 8 and 9.

8. Various space missions (launch) from Cape Canaveral.
(7)

9. Groups (protect) endangered species such as whales.
(7)

10. In the sentence below, circle each proper noun needing a capital letter.
(8)

    (r)uth (h)andler created plastic dolls named (b)arbie in (d)enver (c)olorado.

Circle the simple subject of sentences 11–13.

11. (Skiers) flock to the snow-capped mountains of Colorado.
(3)

12. Are (students) at the university working hard?
(3)

13. Here is a famous seafood (restaurant.)
(3)

Circle the simple predicate of sentences 14–16.

14. Skiers (flock) to the snow-capped mountains of Colorado.
(4)

15. Students at the university (are working) hard.
(4)

16. Here (is) a famous seafood restaurant.
(4)

For 17–19, write whether the word group is a sentence fragment or a complete sentence.

17. Jimmy Carter, our thirty-ninth President ,was born in Georgia. ___complete sentence___
(5)

18. To begin selling peanut butter. ___sentence fragment___
(5)

19. Measuring the enormous span of the pelican's wings. ___sentence fragment___
(5)

20. Draw a vertical line between the subject and predicate parts of the sentence below.
(1)

The 1858 Gold Rush | began in Colorado at Pike's Peak.

Circle the correct word(s) to complete sentences 1–5.

1. The two essential parts of a sentence are the (subordinate, (subject)) and the predicate.
(1)

2. The simple ((subject), predicate) is the main word or words in a sentence that tell who or what is
(3) doing or being something.

3. Norma (carve, (carves)) ice sculptures in Minnesota.
(9)

4. The sentence below is (declarative, (interrogative), exclamatory, imperative).
(2)

Does Michigan have copper mines?

5. The sentence below is a (complete sentence, (sentence fragment)).
(5)

Named for the Indian word meaning great lake.

6. For a–e, circle the correct definition. (1 point for each correct answer)

  (a) An isthmus is a narrow strip of ((land), ocean, water) connecting two larger bodies of land.
(11)

  (b) A (lagoon, (strait), peninsula) is a narrow waterway connecting two larger bodies of water.
(12)

  (c) A (delta, (tributary), archipelago) is a river or stream that flows into a larger river or stream.
(13)

  (d) A (strait, lagoon, (hemisphere)) is one half of the earth.
(14)

  (e) (Meridian, Hemisphere, (Latitude)) is a distance north or south of the equator.
(15)

7. On the lines below, rewrite and correct the sentence fragment, making a complete sentence.
(6)

Fur traders trapping wolverines.

Example: Fur traders were trapping wolverines. (Answers will vary.)

_____

_____

8. Circle the action verb in the sentence below.
(7)

People (nicknamed) Michigan the Wolverine State.

9. In the sentence below, replace the blank with the correct verb form.
(10)

  Chi (past of *shop*) ____shopped____ at the Mall of America in Bloomington, Minnesota.

10. In the sentence below, circle each proper noun needing a capital letter.
(8)

(michigan's) (windmill island municipal park) has an authentic (dutch) windmill.

11. Circle the simple subject in the sentence below.
(3)

Along came (Melody) on a calico horse.

12. Circle the simple predicate in the sentence below.
(4)

Along (came) Melody on a calico horse.

13. Circle the abstract noun in the following list: horse, island (pessimism,) peninsula, wolverine
(11)

14. Circle the word from this list that could *not* be a helping verb: is, am, are, was, were, be (and)
(12)

15. Circle the compound noun from this list: Washington, (afternoon), predicate, optimism
(13)

16. Circle the possessive noun in the sentence below.
(13)

(Minnesota's) prairie has a large gopher population.

Circle each letter that should be capitalized in 17–19.

17. (i) am always amazed at how little (i) know.
(15)

18. (a) famous medical center, (m)ayo (c)linic treats people from all over the world.
(15)

19.   (i) love my red rooster;
(15)   (m)y rooster loves me.
        (i) love my red rooster
        (u)nder the cottonwood tree.

20. Draw a vertical line between the subject and predicate parts of the sentence below.
(1)

A statue of Paul Bunyan | stands in Bemidji, Minnesota.

Circle the correct word(s) to complete sentences 1–5.

1. *John's* is a (possessive, plural) noun.
(13)

2. *Team* is a (compound, collective) noun.
(11)

3. A diamond (scratch, scratches) granite.
(9)

4. The sentence below is (declarative, interrogative, exclamatory, imperative).
(2)

Don't eat too many French fries.

5. The sentence below is a (complete sentence, sentence fragment).
(5)

To build and repair submarines.

6. For a–e, circle the correct definition. (1 point for each correct answer)

(a) A (mesa, plateau, chasm) is a deep, wide crack in the earth's surface.
(20)

(b) (Arroyo, Atoll, Tundra) is a flat, frozen, treeless plain.
(19)

(c) Trees do not grow above the (timber, date, twenty-yard) line.
(18)

(d) The Tropic of Cancer is an imaginary (friend, line, atoll) parallel to the equator.
(17)

(e) A(n) (arroyo, atoll, savanna) is a circular coral reef.
(16)

7. On the lines below, write the four principal parts of the verb *plant*.
(19)

plant	(is) planting	planted	(has) planted
(present tense)	(present participle)	(past tense)	(past participle)

8. Circle the two action verbs in the sentence below.
(7)

Today, people in New Hampshire's shipyards build and repair submarines.

9. In the sentence below, replace the blank with the correct verb form.
(10)

The sculptor (past of *chip*) ____chipped____ the granite.

10. Circle each preposition in the sentence below.
(20)

Without good sense, an explorer ventures into a dark cave.

11. Circle the simple subject in the sentence below.
(3)

On the eastern border of New Hampshire are shipyards.

12. Circle the simple predicate in the sentence below.
(4)

On the eastern border of New Hampshire (are) shipyards.

13. In the sentence below, replace the blank with the correct verb form.
(18)

New Hampshire (past of *be*) _____was_____ the first to declare independence from Great Britain.

14. Circle the word from this list that is *not* a preposition: about, before, by, for, from, (drown)
(20)

15. For a–e, write the plural of each singular noun. (1 point for each correct answer)
(16, 17)

(a) sky _____skies_____

(b) Lewis _____Lewises_____

(c) eggplant _____eggplants_____

(d) loaf _____loaves_____

(e) tooth _____teeth_____

16. Circle the possessive noun in the sentence below.
(13)

Vines covered the (cave's) entrance.

Circle each letter that should be capitalized in 17 and 18.

17. (i) have never read (miss) (pickerell) (goes) to (mars).
(15)

18. (alejandro) will climb (mount) (washington) to the highest point in (new) (england).
(15)

19. Circle the entire verb phrase in the sentence below.
(12)

People in Portsmouth (have been building) ships since 1630.

20. Draw a vertical line between the subject and predicate parts of the sentence below.
(1)

Eva's great-grandfather | planted potatoes in New Hampshire.

Circle the correct word(s) to complete sentences 1–11.

1. (Do, (Did)) Johnny Appleseed plant apple trees in Ohio?
(18)

2. We (will, (shall)) see Ohio's Rock and Roll Hall of Fame tomorrow.
(14)

3. Thomas Edison invented and (perfects, (perfected)) the lightbulb.
(10)

4. The sentence below is ((declarative), interrogative, imperative, exclamatory):
(2)

            The first cash register came from Dayton, Ohio.

5. The following is a (sentence fragment, run-on sentence, (complete sentence)):
(5)

            An ancient dugout canoe was found in Ohio.

6. The word *around* is a (noun, verb, (preposition)).
(20)

7. The noun *lightbulb* is (abstract, (concrete)).
(11)

8. The noun *compass* is ((singular), plural).
(13)

9. To *placate* means to (disturb, anger, (calm)).
(22)

10. To *ignite* is to (disclose, (burn), freeze).
(25)

11. Jenny and Phil marry. Phil (marrys, (marries)) Jenny.
(9)

12. Write the plural form of a–d:
(16, 17)

    (a) tooth __teeth__   (b) cuff __cuffs__   (c) county __counties__   (d) ditch __ditches__

Circle each letter that should be capitalized in 13–15.

13. One sometimes reads of johnny appleseed. His trees still grow around Ohio.
(15)

14. rhett butler remains a popular character from the novel *gone with the wind.*
(25)

15. lake erie forms part of the northern border of Ohio.
(8)

16. Circle each preposition that you find in this sentence:
(20)

      Two of the astronauts, Neil Armstrong and John Glenn, are from the state of Ohio.

17. Circle the two helping verbs in the following sentence:
(12)

Thomas Edison (had)(been) experimenting with electricity for many years.

18. For a–d, circle the correct irregular verb form.
(18)

(a) She (am, (is), are)   (b) They ((do), does)   (c) You (has, (have))   (d) He (do, (does))

19. Complete the four principal parts of the verb *wish*.
(19)

*wish*   *(is)* wishing   wished   *(has)* wished

(1) present tense   (2) present participle   (3) past tense   (4) past participle

20. Circle the simple subject of the sentence below.
(4)

Deep under the ground rested the oldest (watercraft.)

21. Circle the simple predicate of the sentence below.
(4)

Deep under the ground (rested) the oldest watercraft.

22. Write the plural form of the singular noun *commander in chief*.   _commanders in chief_
(22)

23. Circle the action verb in the sentence below.
(7)

The state of Ohio (produces) many tires.

24. Rewrite the following sentence fragment, making a complete sentence.
(6)

To see a tire factory in Ohio.

Example: I would like to see a tire factory in Ohio. (Answers will vary.)

25. Rewrite and correct the run-on sentence below.
(24)

Annie Oakley was born in Ohio she was a famous sharpshooter.

Annie Oakley was born in Ohio. She was a famous sharpshooter.

Give after Lesson 35

Circle the correct word(s) to complete sentences 1–11.

1. (Have, (Has)) the museum opened yet?
(18)

2. We (will, (shall)) see the faces carved on Mount Rushmore.
(14)

3. Nancy went out and (talks, (talked)) to the horses.
(10)

4. The sentence below is (declarative, (interrogative), imperative, exclamatory):
(2)

Did Wild Bill Hickock die in South Dakota?

5. The following is a (sentence fragment, (run-on sentence), complete sentence):
(23)

We saw the Black Hills the trees there look almost black.

6. The word *through* is a (noun, verb, (preposition)).
(21)

7. The noun *peace* is ((abstract), concrete).
(11)

8. The noun *cat's* is (plural, (possessive)).
(13)

9. A large meteorite might create a (mountain, (crater), hill) on the earth's surface.
(29)

10. A(n) (meteorite, caldera, (etymology)) shows a word's original language and meaning.
(30)

11. Chickens scratch. A chicken (scratch, (scratches)).
(9)

12. Write the plural form of a–d:
(16, 17)

    (a) knife __knives__   (b) monkey __monkeys__ (c) cupful __cupfuls__   (d) entry __entries__

Circle each letter that should be capitalized in 13–15.

13. (l)ilah said, "(t)hat (n)orth (d)akota blizzard was terrible."
(26)

14. (o)n (s)aturday we shall read (a)lice in (w)onderland.
(25)

15. (l)ake (o)ntario forms part of the northern border of (n)ew (y)ork.
(8)

16. Circle each preposition that you find in the sentence below.
(20, 21)

    (Since) yesterday, the explorer has been (inside) the cave (by) himself, (without) a buddy.

17. Circle the two helping verbs in the following sentence:
(12)

Clara Barton (had)(been) nursing the wounded for three years.

18. For a–d, circle the correct irregular verb form.
(18)

(a) They (am, is, (are))   (b) She (do, (does))   (c) He ((has), have)   (d) You ((do), does)

19. Complete the four principal parts of the verb *try*.
(19)

try	*(is)* trying	tried	*(has)* tried
(1) present tense	(2) present participle	(3) past tense	(4) past participle

20. Circle the simple subject of the sentence below.
(4)

Out on the range roams a (herd) of buffalo.

21. Circle the simple predicate of the sentence below.
(4)

Out on the range (roams) a herd of buffalo.

22. Write the plural form of the singular noun *father-in-law*.   fathers-in-law
(22)

23. Draw a vertical line between the subject and the predicate of the sentence below.
(1)

Wild Bill Hickok and Wyatt Earp | chased outlaws in the Wild West.

24. Circle each silent letter in the words below.
(28, 29)

(a) (h)our   (b) ri(d)ge   (c) wa(l)k   (d) de(b)t

25. Rewrite and correct the run-on sentence below.
(24)

South Dakota is the Mount Rushmore State its capital is Pierre.

South Dakota is the Mount Rushmore State. Its capital is Pierre.

Circle the correct word(s) to complete sentences 1–10.

1. Etymologies are (antonyms, synonyms, (word histories)).
(30)

2. George Washington ((was), were) born in Virginia.
(18)

3. Stephen stepped outide and (calls, (called)) his dog.
(10)

4. The sentence below is (declarative, interrogative, imperative, (exclamatory)):
(2)

The musical was fabulous!

5. The following is a ((sentence fragment,) run-on sentence, complete sentence):
(5)

Buried treasure in the Mojave Desert.

6. The word *at* is a (noun, verb, (preposition)).
(21)

7. The noun *backpack* is (abstract, (concrete)).
(11)

8. The noun *cats* is ((plural), possessive).
(13)

9. The verb ((look), laugh, smile) is a common linking verb.
(31)

10. Many people watch. One person (watch, (watches)).
(9)

11. For a–d, circle the correct definition. (1 point for each correct answer)

    (a) ((Kin), Clamor, Panacea) refers to one's relatives.
    (35)

    (b) A (kin, (clamor), panacea) is a loud cry or uproar.
    (34)

    (c) (Clamor, (Indispensable), Dispensable) means absolutely necessary.
    (33)

    (d) The Greek root *pan* means (fire, table, (all)).
    (32)

12. Write the plural form of a–d:
(16, 17)

    (a) suffix __suffixes__   (b) inch __inches__   (c) dairy __dairies__   (d) deer __deer__

Circle each letter that should be capitalized in 13–15.

13. (m)rs. (n)g asked, "(h)ave you seen (m)eg's other shoe?"
(26)

14. (p)lease read me "(t)he (c)at in the (h)at."
(25)

15. (the) (mississippi) (river) forms the eastern border of (arkansas).
(8)

16. Circle each preposition that you find in the sentence below.
(20, 21)

(Over) this hill and (across) the field lies a grove (of) apple trees (with) many blossoms.

17. For a–d, circle the word that is spelled correctly. (1 point for each correct answer)
(33-35)

    (a) (weigh), wiegh   (b) decieve, (deceive)   (c) forgeting, (forgetting) (d) (countries,) countrys

18. For a–d, circle the correct irregular verb form. (1 point for each correct answer)
(18)

    (a) He (am, (is,) are)   (b) I ((am,) is, are)   (c) She ((has,) have)   (d) It (do, (does))

19. Complete the four principal parts of the verb *flap*.
(19)

flap	*(is)* flapping	flapped	*(has)* flapped
(1) present tense	(2) present participle	(3) past tense	(4) past participle

20. Add suffixes. (2 points for each correct answer)
(33)

    (a) dry + est   driest   (b) say + ed   said

21. Add suffixes. (2 points for each correct answer)
(34)

    (a) glad + ly   gladly   (b) begin + ing   beginning

22. From the following list, circle the word that could *not* be a linking verb: is, am, are, (wash) were
(31)

23. Circle each silent letter in the words below. (1 point for each correct answer)
(28, 29)

    (a) (w)ho   (b) rece(p)t   (c) lam(b)   (d) clim(b)

On the lines provided, diagram the simple subject and simple predicate of sentences 24 and 25.

24. Across the desert gallops an Arabian horse.
(32)

    horse | gallops

25. Has the stallion seen the mare?
(32)

    stallion | Has seen

Circle the correct word(s) to complete sentences 1–10.

1. ((Etymologies), Atolls, Peninsulas) are word histories.
(30)

2. (Do (Does)) she like jazz music?
(18)

3. A muddy beagle (follows, (followed)) me home yesterday.
(10)

4. The word group below is a ((phrase), clause):
(36)

throughout the state of Washington

5. The following is a (sentence fragment, (run-on sentence), complete sentence):
(23)

Nevada gets very little rain it is mostly desert.

6. The word *across* is a (noun, verb, (preposition)).
(20)

7. The noun *miracle* is ((abstract), concrete).
(11)

8. The noun *Jameses* is ((plural), possessive).
(13)

9. The verb (wait, (seem), stare) is a common linking verb.
(31)

10. Sodas fizz. A soda (fizzs, (fizzes)).
(9)

11. For a–d, circle the correct definition. (1 point for each correct answer)

(a) A ((dogmatic), timid, humble) person speaks with authority and sometimes arrogance.
(39)

(b) To humiliate is to shame or (exalt, praise, (embarrass)).
(38)

(c) A heavy load might (encourage, enable, (encumber)) a traveler.
(37)

(d) Avarice is (generosity, (greed), patience).
(36)

12. Write the plural form of a–d:
(16, 17)

(a) fax __faxes__   (b) dish __dishes__   (c) baby __babies__   (d) child __children__

Circle each letter that should be capitalized in 13–15.

13. (a)ddicus asked, "(d)id you find that book on (m)s. (b)lue's bookshelf?"
(26)

14. (m)ay (i) borrow your copy of (a)lice in (w)onderland?
(25)

15. $\widehat{I}$ offered $\widehat{ms.}$ $\widehat{hoo}$ some hot $\widehat{french}$ bread.
(38)

16. Circle each preposition that you find in the sentence below.
(20, 21)

$\widehat{Without}$ your help, I could not have rescued my horse $\widehat{from}$ the flood.

17. For a–d, circle the word that is spelled correctly. (1 point for each correct answer)
(33-35)

(a) nieghbor $\widehat{neighbor}$ (b) $\widehat{priest}$, preist (c) runing $\widehat{running}$ (d) librarys $\widehat{libraries}$

18. Circle each limiting adjective in the sentence below.
(40)

$\widehat{Fernando's}$ band has $\widehat{a}$ drummer $\widehat{a}$ pianist, and $\widehat{two}$ guitarists.

19. Complete the four principal parts of the verb *reply*.
(19)

reply	*(is)* replying	replied	*(has)* replied
(1) present tense	(2) present participle	(3) past tense	(4) past participle

20. Add suffixes. (2 points for each correct answer)
(33, 34)

(a) win + ing _____winning_____ (b) pay + ed _____paid_____

21. Circle each descriptive adjective in the sentence below.
(39)

$\widehat{Lush}$ $\widehat{colorful}$ trees in $\widehat{beautiful}$ Vermont attract $\widehat{appreciative}$ spectators.

22. From the following list, circle the word that could *not* be a linking verb: seem, appear, $\widehat{blow}$ stay
(31)

23. Circle each silent letter in the words below. (1 point for each correct answer)
(28, 29)

(a) si$\widehat{g}$n (b) $\widehat{h}$onor (c) lis$\widehat{t}$en (d) lim$\widehat{b}$

On the lines provided, diagram each word of sentences 24 and 25.

24. My puppy has chewed my new shoes.
(32)

```
  puppy  |  has chewed  |  shoes
 \My           \my  \new
```

25. Has that puppy chewed your new shoes?
(32)

```
  puppy  |  Has chewed  |  shoes
 \that          \your  \new
```

Circle the correct word(s) to complete sentences 1–10.

1. (Field labels, (Etymologies,) Antonyms) are word histories showing the original language and meaning.
(30)

2. West Virginia (have, (has)) many coal mines.
(18)

3. Settlers followed the trail and (arrive, (arrived)) in West Virginia.
(10)

4. The word group below is a (phrase, (clause)):
(36)

         because it lies in the Appalachian Mountain system

5. The following is a ((sentence fragment,) run-on sentence, complete sentence):
(5)

         Jamestown, the first permanent English colony.

6. The word *the* is a (noun, verb, (adjective,) preposition).
(40)

7. The noun *success* is ((abstract,) concrete).
(11)

8. The noun *James's* is (plural, (possessive)).
(13)

9. The verb (think, sing, (was)) is a common linking verb.
(31)

10. Bees buzz. A bee (buzzs, (buzzes)).
(9)

11. For a–d, circle the correct definition. (1 point for each correct answer)

    (a) (Frugal, (Cognizant,) Paternal) means having knowledge; aware.
(41)

    (b) An imprudent decision is (frugal, (unwise,) wise).
(44)

    (c) ((Frugal,) Cognizant, Paternal) means avoiding waste.
(42)

    (d) (Frugal, Cognizant, (Paternal)) means of or like a father.
(43)

12. Write the plural form of a–d:
(16, 17)

    (a) loaf __loaves__   (b) cupful __cupfuls__   (c) man __men__   (d) piano __pianos__

Circle each letter that should be capitalized in 13–15.

13. (d)aniel explained, "(w)est (v)irginia was once a part of (v)irginia."
(26)

14. "(u)nfortunately, diseases such as measles, mumps, and chicken pox caused the deaths of many (n)ative (a)mericans," said (d)aniel.
(43)

15. dear grandma,
(38, 41)
      have you visited the east?
          love,
          genevie

16. Circle each preposition that you find in the sentence below.
(20, 21)

West Virginia sided (with) the North (during) the Civil War.

17. Circle the misspelled word in the list below.
(33-35)

relieve, height, (wiegh) eight, deceive

18. Circle each adjective in the sentence below.
(39, 40)

(Prudent) students will do (the) homework.

19. Complete the four principal parts of the verb *drop*.
(19)

drop	*(is)* dropping	dropped	*(has)* dropped
(1) present tense	(2) present participle	(3) past tense	(4) past participle

20. Add suffixes. (2 points for each correct answer)
(33, 34)

(a) clap + ing   clapping   (b) pretty + er   prettier

21. In the sentence below, underline the prepositional phrase and circle the object of the preposition.
(44)

Did she tell you the secret <u>of her (success)</u>?

22. Circle the proper adjective in the sentence below.
(42)

Jamestown was the first permanent (English) colony.

23. Circle each silent letter in the words below. (1 point for each correct answer)
(28, 29)

(a) cu(p)board   (b) ta(l)k   (c) (g)uess   (d) com(b)

On the lines provided, diagram each word of sentences 24 and 25.

24. Do you eat a variety of healthful foods?
(40, 45)

25. A prudent student will do the homework.
(40)

Circle the correct word(s) to complete sentences 1–10.

1. The boldfaced word that begins a dictionary entry gives the (etymology, part of speech, (spelling)).
(27)

2. Terry (do, (does)) the homework.
(18)

3. He unlocked the treasure chest and (looks, (looked)) inside.
(10)

4. The word group below is a ((phrase), clause):
(36)

        six feet long with mossy, leathery skin, the alligator

5. The following is a (sentence fragment, run-on sentence, (complete sentence)):
(5, 23)

        The man at the piano is Duke Ellington.

6. The word *an* is a (noun, verb, (adjective) preposition).
(40)

7. The noun *alligator* is (abstract, (concrete)).
(11)

8. The noun *alligators* is ((plural), possessive).
(13)

9. The verb (whisper, sneeze, (smell)) is a common linking verb.
(31)

10. Birds fly. A bird (flys, (flies)).
(9)

11. For a–d, circle the correct definition. (1 point for each correct answer)

    (a) ((Illiterate), Frugal, Benevolent) means unable to read or write.
    (46)

    (b) A (Plausible, (Momentous), Intolerable) occasion is one of great importance.
    (47)

    (c) A believable story is (frugal, intolerable, (plausible)).
    (48)

    (d) Benevolent means ((kind), believable, unbearable).
    (50)

12. Add periods as needed: I. Washington D. C.
(47, 50)   A. The White House
                                 B. The Capitol Building

Circle each letter that should be capitalized in 13 and 14.

13. nolan asked, "may i borrow your book about georgia?"
(26)

14. dear gavin,
(38, 41)   your grandfather owned land in the midwest and in the south.
              love,
              aunt bessie

15. Circle the linking verb in the sentence below.
(31)

That Georgian peach (smells) so sweet!

16. Circle each coordinating conjunction in the sentence below.
(48)

He toured the White House (and) the Capitol Building, (but) she went to the Smithsonian Museum.

17. Circle the misspelled word in the list below.
(33-35)

believe, (nieghbor), weigh, niece

18. Circle each adjective in the sentence below.
(39, 40)

(Two) (sleepy) alligators lie in (the) (hot) sun.

19. Complete the four principal parts of the verb *cry*.
(19)

cry	*(is)* crying	cried	*(has)* cried
(1) present tense	(2) present participle	(3) past tense	(4) past participle

20. Add suffixes. (2 points for each correct answer)
(33, 34)

(a) trap + ed _____trapped_____   (b) cloudy + er _____cloudier_____

21. In the sentence below, underline each prepositional phrase, circling the object of each preposition.
(44)

Lucas looks <u>down the basketball (court)</u> and sprints <u>to the (basket)</u>.

22. Circle the proper adjective in the sentence below.
(42)

Does Fido like (Swiss) cheese?

23. Circle the indirect object in the sentence below.
(46)

The benevolent couple gave stray (dogs) food and shelter.

On the lines provided, diagram each word of sentences 24 and 25.

24. Did the man at the piano play classical music?
(40, 45)

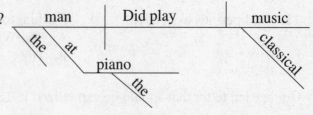

25. Joe and Moe repair and polish old bikes.
(40, 49)

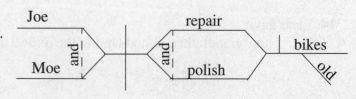

Circle the correct word(s) to complete sentences 1–10.

1. Of the two buildings, this one is (**taller**, tallest).
(55)

2. Terry (have, **has**) two brothers.
(18)

3. She closed the window and (locks, **locked**) the door.
(10)

4. The word group below is a (phrase, **clause**):
(36)
> if you see an alligator with an open mouth

5. The following is a (**sentence fragment**, run-on sentence, complete sentence):
(5)
> Duke Ellington, the man at the piano.

6. The word *the* is a (noun, verb, **adjective**, preposition).
(40)

7. The noun *optimism* is (**abstract**, concrete).
(11)

8. The noun *alligator's* is (plural, **possessive**).
(13)

9. The verb (honk, clap, **sound**) is a common linking verb.
(31)

10. Students *try* hard. A student (trys, **tries**) hard.
(9)

11. For a–d, circle the correct definition. (1 point for each correct answer)

  (a) (Bovine, **Canine**, Feline) relates to dogs.
  (51)

  (b) (**Bovine**, Canine, Equine) relates to cows.
  (52)

  (c) Auditory relates to the sense of (smell, **hearing**, touch).
  (53)

  (d) Gentility is (malice, **courtesy**, greed).
  (55)

12. Add periods as needed in the sentence below.
(47, 50)
> Mr. Brite wrote, "The First Ave. market will be closed Tues. this week."

Circle each letter that should be capitalized in 13 and 14.

13. mimi said, "some crops in the south are harvested in spring."
(26)

14. dear alsumana,
(38, 41)
> do you have rollercoasters in papua new guinea? i like fast and twisty ones.
> your friend,
> elisa

15. Circle the predicate nominative in the sentence below.
(51)

Mrs. Cruz is a prudent (attorney)

16. Circle each coordinating conjunction in the sentence below.
(48)

Ian (and) Rosa are visiting North (or) South Carolina, (but) their home is in Florida.

17. Circle the misspelled word in the list below.
(33-35)

(beleive) neighbor, weigh, niece

18. Circle each adjective in the sentence below.
(39, 40)

(Four) (fuzzy) rabbits hide inside (a) (hollow) log.

19. Complete the four principal parts of the verb *trap*.
(19)

<u>*trap*</u>	<u>*(is)* trapping</u>	<u>trapped</u>	<u>*(has)* trapped</u>
(1) present tense	(2) present participle	(3) past tense	(4) past participle

20. Add suffixes. (2 points for each correct answer)
(33, 34)

(a) cry + ed _____cried_____   (b) happy + est _____happiest_____

21. In the sentence below, underline each prepositional phrase, circling the object of each
(44) preposition.

A dog <u>with a rhinestone (collar)</u> leaps <u>into the (car)</u>

22. Circle the proper adjective in the sentence below.
(42)

Juicy (California) oranges make a good snack.

23. Circle the indirect object in the sentence below.
(46)

Hnin passed (Borden) the baton.

On the lines provided, diagram each word of sentences 24 and 25.

24. The man at the piano is my brother.
(45, 51)

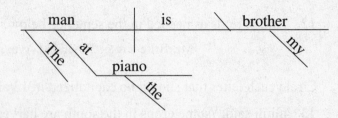

25. Joe and Moe wash and wax their car.
(40, 49)

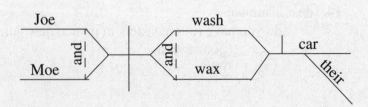

Circle the correct word(s) to complete sentences 1–10.

1. Of the two computers, this one is (better, best).
(56)

2. We (was, were) friends.
(18)

3. Yesterday he (fry, fries, fried) potatoes.
(10)

4. The word group below is a (phrase, clause):
(36)
　　　　　instead of the movie about pirates

5. The following is a (sentence fragment, run-on sentence, complete sentence):
(23, 24)
　　　　　The truck swerved it hit a curb.

6. A(n) (declarative, interrogative, imperative, exclamatory) sentence asks a question.
(2)

7. The noun *elephant* is (abstract, concrete).
(11)

8. I have two (sister-in-laws, sisters-in-law).
(13, 16)

9. The verb (touch, grab, feel) is a common linking verb.
(31)

10. Bees *buzz*. A bee (buzzs, buzzes).
(9)

11. For a–d, circle the correct definition. (1 point for each correct answer)

　(a) (Intangible, Superfluous, Malicious) means more than needed or desired.
　(58)

　(b) (Opportune, Inopportune, Indolent) means suitable; well-timed.
　(60)

　(c) Indolent means (lazy, generous, hard-working).
　(56)

　(d) To illuminate is to give (food, money, light) to.
　(59)

12. Add periods as needed in the sentence below.
(47, 50)
　　　　Mrs. Lynch's note reads, "Buy two lbs. of apples at the Main St. market."

Circle each letter that should be capitalized in 13 and 14.

13. ms. hoo said, "some states in the east are humid in summer."
(26)

14. dear rafael,
(38, 41)
　　　are there alligators in tallahassee, florida? i hope not.
　　　　　your friend,
　　　　　josef

15. Add commas as needed in the sentence below.
(59, 60)

Ms. Hoo**,** I would like you to meet my mother**,** Mrs. Chavez.

16. Circle each coordinating conjunction in the sentence below.
(48)

I ordered soup (and) salad, (for) I was hungry.

17. Circle the misspelled word in the list below.
(33-35)

neighbor, weigh, view, (veiw)

18. Circle the antecedent of the italicized pronoun in the sentence below.
(62)

(Leo) left *his* skateboard outside.

19. Complete the four principal parts of the verb *wrap*.
(19)

wrap	_(is)_ wrapping	wrapped	_(has)_ wrapped
(1) present tense	(2) present participle	(3) past tense	(4) past participle

20. Add suffixes. (2 points for each correct answer)
(33, 34)

(a) give + ing ___giving___   (b) pretty + er ___prettier___

21. In the sentence below, underline each prepositional phrase, circling the object of each
(44) preposition.

The cheese <u>on the (table)</u> comes <u>from (Wisconsin)</u>

22. Circle the proper adjective in the sentence below.
(42)

Please slice some (Wisconsin) cheese for sandwiches.

23. Circle the indirect object in the sentence below.
(46)

He handed (me) an envelope.

On the lines provided, diagram each word of sentences 24 and 25.

24. The trip was expensive but worthwhile.
(49, 54)

25. The little boat on the lake endured a big storm.
(40, 45)

Circle the correct word(s) to complete sentences 1–10.

1. You made (less, (fewer)) mistakes than I did.
(56)

2. After the test, we (was, (were)) elated.
(18)

3. The pronoun *he* is (first, second, (third)) person.
(64)

4. The word group below is a (phrase, (clause)):
(36)
                    for they produce breakfast cereal

5. The following is a ((sentence fragment), run-on sentence, complete sentence):
(5, 23)
                    Raising hogs in both Indiana and Illinois.

6. The hardy tree ((grew,) grown) quickly.
(65)

7. The noun *tenacity* is ((abstract,) concrete).
(11)

8. She has two (brother-in-laws, (brothers-in-law)).
(13, 16)

9. The verb (sing, speak, (were)) is a common linking verb.
(31)

10. Julia has (wore, (worn)) out her socks.
(65)

11. For a–d, circle the correct definition. (1 point for each correct answer)

(a) (Gentility, (Intuition,) Pessimism) is an instinctive feeling or knowledge.
(61)

(b) Cowardice is lack of (food, money, (courage)).
(62)

(c) One who is ((tenacious,) malicious, indolent) does not give up.
(63)

(d) ((Ethical,) Unethical, Intrepid) means morally right.
(64)

12. Add periods as needed in the sentence below.
(47, 50)
         Mr. Cross paid $1.99 (one dollar and ninety-nine cents) for four lbs. of bananas.

13. Circle each letter that should be capitalized in the sentence below.
(42, 43)
                    a (b)ritish musician played the (f)rench horn skillfully.

14. For a–d, write the plural of each noun.
(16, 22)

(a) dish __dishes__   (b) monkey __monkeys__

(c) baby __babies__   (d) spoonful __spoonfuls__

15. Add commas as needed in the sentence below.
(59, 60)

Ms. Hoo, I would like you to meet my mother, Mrs. Chavez.

16. Circle each coordinating conjunction in the sentence below.
(48)

I ordered soup (and) salad, (for) I was hungry.

17. Circle the misspelled word in the list below.
(33-35)

neighbor, weigh, view, (veiw)

18. Circle the antecedent of the italicized pronoun in the sentence below.
(62)

(Leo) left *his* skateboard outside.

19. Complete the four principal parts of the verb *wrap*.
(19)

wrap	*(is)* wrapping	wrapped	*(has)* wrapped
(1) present tense	(2) present participle	(3) past tense	(4) past participle

20. Add suffixes. (2 points for each correct answer)
(33, 34)

(a) give + ing ____giving____　　(b) pretty + er ____prettier____

21. In the sentence below, underline each prepositional phrase, circling the object of each preposition.
(44)

The cheese <u>on the (table)</u> comes <u>from (Wisconsin)</u>

22. Circle the proper adjective in the sentence below.
(42)

Please slice some (Wisconsin) cheese for sandwiches.

23. Circle the indirect object in the sentence below.
(46)

He handed (me) an envelope.

On the lines provided, diagram each word of sentences 24 and 25.

24. The trip was expensive but worthwhile.
(49, 54)

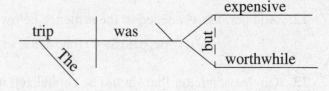

25. The little boat on the lake endured a big storm.
(40, 45)

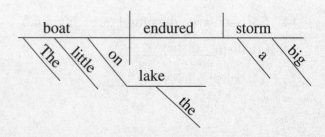

Circle the correct word(s) to complete sentences 1–10.

1. I have eaten (less, (fewer)) tacos than she has.
(56)

2. Doreen went to Yosemite with Austin and (I, (me)).
(70)

3. The pronoun *you* is (first, (second), third) person.
(64)

4. The word group below is a ((phrase), clause):
(36)

　　　　　　a locomotive and many passenger cars at the station

5. The following is a ((sentence fragment), run-on sentence, complete sentence):
(23, 24)

　　　　　　The long, lonesome whistle of the steam train.

6. Vintage Shay locomotives have (blow, blew, (blown)) their whistles for decades.
(65)

7. The comparative form of the adjective *bad* is (bad, (worse), worst).
(55, 56)

8. The word *brother-in-law's* is a (plural, (possessive)) noun.
(13)

9. The verb ((seemed), said, whispered) is a common linking verb.
(31)

10. Julia has (drank, (drunk)) eight glasses of water today.
(65)

11. For a–d, circle the correct definition. (1 point for each correct answer)

　(a) Ornithology is the study of (weather, rocks, (birds)).
　(68)

　(b) To feign is to ((pretend), listen, travel).
　(69)

　(c) (Intrepid, Tenacious, (Contrite)) means sorry.
　(66)

　(d) (Irrelevant, (Pertinent), Contrite) means relevant or applicable.
　(67)

12. Add periods as needed in the sentence below.
(47, 50)

　　　　　　At two a.m. Ms. Overwork finally finished her essay.

13. Circle each letter that should be capitalized in the sentence below.
(42, 43)

　　　　　　(i)n the (e)ast, (i)talian (a)mericans settled to begin a new life.

14. For a–d, write the plural of each noun.
(16, 22)

　(a) bench __benches__ 　　　　　(b) donkey __donkeys__

　(c) cherry __cherries__ 　　　　　(d) cupful __cupfuls__

15. Add commas as needed to clarify the sentence below.
(68)

With Lucy, Thomas writes well.

16. Circle each coordinating conjunction in the sentence below.
(48)

I have no pen (or) pencil, (yet) I have plenty of paper.

17. Circle the misspelled word in the list below.
(33-35)

neighbor, weigh, (reciept), receipt

18. Circle the antecedent of the italicized pronoun in the sentence below.
(62)

(Sharon) carries *her* heavy backpack for miles.

19. Complete the four principal parts of the verb *grow*.
(19)

<u>grow</u>	<u>*(is)* growing</u>	<u>grew</u>	<u>*(has)* grown</u>
(1) present tense	(2) present participle	(3) past tense	(4) past participle

20. Add suffixes. (2 points for each correct answer)
(33, 34)

(a) hope + ing <u>   hoping   </u>   (b) sunny + est <u>   sunniest   </u>

21. In the sentence below, underline each prepositional phrase, circling the object of each preposition.
(44)

The train <u>at the (station)</u> will soon leave <u>for (Chicago)</u>.

22. Circle the proper adjective in the sentence below.
(42)

How many (Georgia) peaches are in this pie?

23. Circle the indirect object in the sentence below.
(46, 69)

The ranger gave (us) a tour of the area.

On the lines provided, diagram each word of sentences 24 and 25.

24. Your brother seems tenacious and ethical.
(49, 54)

25. The rabbit in the garden ate two ripe melons.
(40, 45)

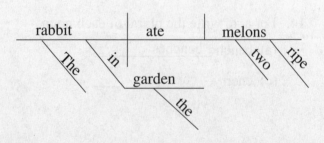

Circle the correct word(s) to complete sentences 1–10.

1. Anita is the (**better**, best) of the two guitarists.
(56)

2. The geology experts were Rocky and (her, **she**).
(66)

3. The pronoun *we* is (**first**, second, third) person.
(64)

4. The clause below is (**dependent**, independent):
(73)
when minerals form around geyser vents

5. The following is a (sentence fragment, **run-on sentence**, complete sentence):
(23, 24)
The geyser is quiet it will erupt soon.

6. The ship (sink, **sank**, sunk) long ago.
(65)

7. The superlative form of the adjective *bad* is (bad, worse, **worst**).
(55, 56)

8. The sentence below is (simple, **compound**):
(75)
The geyser blew, and I ran for cover!

9. The verb (**looks**, says, sings) is a common linking verb.
(31)

10. Norm has (break, broke, **broken**) his arm again.
(65)

11. For a–d, circle the correct definition. (1 point for each correct answer)

(a) (Serene, Ethical, **Ardent**) means passionate and zealous.
(71)

(b) Serene means (angry, troubled, **peaceful**).
(72)

(c) Sagacity is (**wisdom**, sorrow, trouble).
(73)

(d) (**Redundancy**, Linguistics, Serenity) is needless repetition.
(74)

12. Add periods as needed in the sentence below.
(47, 50)
Mrs. Starlyn saw the geyser's six p.m. eruption.

13. Circle each letter that should be capitalized in the sentence below.
(42, 43)
(C)an (I) buy (I)talian suasage in (n)ew (y)ork?

14. For a–d, write the plural of each noun.
(16, 22)

(a) lunch __lunches__ (b) key __keys__

(c) berry __berries__ (d) handful __handfuls__

15. Add commas as needed in the sentence below.
(68)

When Old Faithful erupts**,** I shall take pictures of it.

16. Circle the coordinating conjunction in the compound sentence below.
(75)

We have been watching (but) the geyser has not blown.

17. Circle the misspelled word in the list below.
(33-35)

neighbor, weigh, piece (peice)

18. Circle the antecedent of the italicized pronoun in the sentence below.
(62)

Although *he* has studied geology, (Clark) cannot explain everything.

19. Complete the four principal parts of the verb *freeze*.
(65)

freeze   *(is)* freezing   froze   *(has)* frozen

(1) present tense   (2) present participle   (3) past tense   (4) past participle

20. Add suffixes. (2 points for each correct answer)
(33, 34)

(a) snap + ed _____snapped_____   (b) argue + ment _____argument_____

21. In the sentence below, underline each prepositional phrase, circling the object of each
(44)   preposition.

A man with an (umbrella) stood beside (me)

22. Circle the predicate nominative in the sentence below.
(51)

Old Faithful is a magnificent (geyser)

23. Circle the indirect object in the sentence below.
(46, 69)

Alberto handed (Quan) a photo.

On the lines provided, diagram each word of sentences 24 and 25.

24. The eruption was sudden and spectacular.
(49, 54)

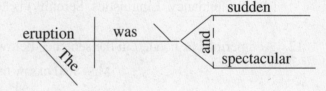

25. The man with the umbrella has two children.
(40, 45)

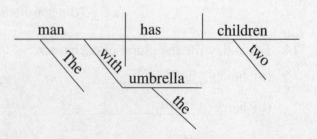

Circle the correct word(s) to complete sentences 1–10.

1. Of the two kittens, that one is (fuzzier, fuzziest).
(56)

2. You know more than (me, I) about prairie dogs.
(78)

3. The pronoun *him* is (nominative, objective, possessive) case.
(66, 69)

4. The clause below is (dependent, independent):
(73)

coyotes threaten the prairie dog colony

5. The following is a (sentence fragment, run-on sentence, complete sentence):
(5, 23)

Burrowing to escape the golden eagle.

6. A prairie dog hides in (it's, its) burrow.
(72)

7. A coyote snarls at Rocky and (he, him).
(69, 70)

8. The sentence below is (simple, compound):
(75)

The prairie dog stopped and looked at me.

9. The man (who, which) counts prairie dogs rides a horse.
(77)

10. Norm has (tear, tore, torn) his shirt again.
(65)

11. For a–d, circle the correct definition. (1 point for each correct answer)

(a) (Dauntless, Quaint, Ardent) means attractive in an old-fashioned way.
(76)

(b) To ameliorate is to (destroy, improve, harm).
(77)

(c) Dauntless means (afraid, heroic, weak).
(79)

(d) (Redundancy, Salinity, Serenity) is saltiness.
(78)

12. Add periods as needed in the sentence below. (4 periods)
(47, 50)

Cherries cost $2.99 (two dollars and ninety-nine cents) per lb., so I bought only eight oz. today.

13. Circle each letter that should be capitalized in the sentence below.
(42, 43)

can i purchase alaskan crab in maine?

14. For a–d, write the plural of each noun.
(16, 22)

(a) bunch ___bunches___   (b) toy ___toys___

(c) colony ___colonies___   (d) mouthful ___mouthfuls___

15. Add commas and quotation marks as needed in the sentence below.
(76, 80)

"After lunch," said Ms. Hoo, "we shall discuss the Utah prairie dog."

16. Circle the coordinating conjunction in the compound sentence below.
(75)

Some prairie dogs are hiding, (for) hawks are circling above.

17. Circle the subordinating conjunction in the sentence below.
(73)

(Because) prairie dogs are social animals, they live together in large colonies.

18. Circle the antecedent of the italicized pronoun in the sentence below.
(62)

Mimi likes (prairie dogs) because *they* are cute.

19. Complete the four principal parts of the verb *steal*.
(65)

steal	*(is)* stealing	stole	*(has)* stolen
(1) present tense	(2) present participle	(3) past tense	(4) past participle

20. Add suffixes. (2 points for each correct answer)
(33, 34)

(a) win + er ___winner___   (b) salty + ness ___saltiness___

21. Circle the interrogative pronoun in the sentence below.
(79)

(Which) shall we study first?

22. Circle the predicate nominative in the sentence below.
(51)

The Utah prairie dog is an endangered (species.)

23. Circle the indirect object in the sentence below.
(46, 69)

Elle made (Daisy) a taco.

On the lines provided, diagram each word of sentences 24 and 25.

24. Prairie dogs are rodents with short tails.
(45, 54)

Prairie dogs | are \ rodents
with
short
tails

25. Max is listening, but Perlina is napping.
(40, 45)

Max | is listening
but
Perlina | is napping

Circle the correct word(s) to complete sentences 1–10.

1. That planet is the (bigger, biggest) of the two.
(56)

2. I am shorter than (he, him).
(78)

3. The pronoun *his* is (nominative, objective, possessive) case.
(70, 72)

4. The clause below is (dependent, independent):
(73)

> since the moon is full tonight

5. One of the students (give, gives) (their, his or her) report each morning.
(83)

6. (Your, You're) car is fast, but (ours, our's) is faster.
(72)

7. A bear watches Grace and (she, her).
(69, 70)

8. The sentence below is (simple, compound):
(75)

> The sky is cloudy, so I cannot see the stars.

9. The woman (who, which) owns the telescope can identify many stars.
(77)

10. (Them, Those) photographs show the solar eclipse.
(82)

11. For a–d, circle the correct definition. (1 point for each correct answer)

(a) A (docent, curator, culprit) is a guilty one.
(81)

(b) Bliss is great (sorrow, happiness, pain).
(82)

(c) (Subversion, Rapport, Rapprochement) is destruction.
(83)

(d) (Subversion, Rapport, Quaintness) is harmony in a relationship.
(84)

12. Add periods as needed in the sentence below. (4 periods)
(47, 50)

> Mrs. Vega lives on S. First St. in Denver.

13. Circle each letter that should be capitalized in the sentence below.
(42, 43)

> will i find washington apples in florida?

14. For a–d, write the plural of each noun.
(16, 22)

(a) branch ___branches___   (b) day ___days___

(c) company ___companies___   (d) child ___children___

15. Add commas and quotation marks as needed in the sentence below.
(76, 80)

"Next week," said Ms. Hoo, "we shall view a solar eclipse."

16. Circle the coordinating conjunction in the compound sentence below.
(75)

The moon is a cold, rocky body, (and) it has no light of its own.

17. Circle the subordinating conjunction in the sentence below.
(73)

The moon appears luminous (because) sunlight reflects from the moon's surface.

18. Circle the antecedent of the italicized pronoun in the sentence below.
(62)

Tex gazed at the (moon) until clouds covered *it*.

19. Complete the four principal parts of the verb *catch*.
(85)

catch	*(is)* catching	caught	*(has)* caught
(1) present tense	(2) present participle	(3) past tense	(4) past participle

20. Add suffixes. (2 points for each correct answer)
(33, 34)

(a) begin + er __beginner__   (b) happy + ness __happiness__

21. Underline the words that should be italicized in the sentence below.
(84)

Someday I shall read Melville's novel, Moby Dick.

22. Circle the predicate nominative in the sentence below.
(51)

That solar eclipse was an awesome (spectacle)

23. Circle the indirect object in the sentence below.
(46, 69)

Did Fido leave (her) any dog food?

On the lines provided, diagram each word of sentences 24 and 25.

24. Is Saturn the planet with rings?
(45, 54)

Saturn | Is \ planet
the \ with
rings

25. Cora and she sew their own clothes.
(40, 71)

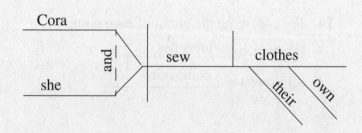

Circle the correct word(s) to complete sentences 1–10.

1. That cave is the (bigger, (biggest)) of all!
(56)

2. Are you as courageous as (me, (I))?
(78)

3. The pronoun *she* is ((nominative), objective, possessive) case.
(70, 72)

4. The clause below is (dependent, (independent)):
(73)
  stalactites and stalagmites decorate the caverns

5. Each of the bats (flap, (flaps)) (their, (its)) wings.
(83)

6. ((They're, (Their), There)) lawn is greener than (her's, (hers)).
(72)

7. This vase of flowers (need, (needs)) water.
(90)

8. The sentence below is ((simple), compound)):
(75)
  Inside the dark cave, bats sleep during the daytime.

9. The people ((who), which) entered the cave have not come out!
(77)

10. Neither the flowers nor the lawn (have, (has)) been watered.
(89)

11. For a–d, circle the correct definition. (1 point for each correct answer)

  (a) Colossal means extremely (small, skinny, (large)).
  (86)

  (b) To (languish, daunt, (coerce)) is to force.
  (87)

  (c) (Colossal, (Complacent), Languid) means content; self-satisfied.
  (88)

  (d) To ((languish), daunt, coerce) is to grow weak.
  (89)

12. Add periods as needed in the sentence below. (4 periods)
(47, 50)
  That library in St. George opens at nine a.m. on Saturdays.

13. Circle each letter that should be capitalized in the sentence below.
(42, 43)
  (c)an we buy (w)isconsin cheese in (n)ew (m)exico?

14. For a–d, write the plural of each noun.
(16, 22)
  (a) bush ___bushes___   (b) valley ___valleys___

  (c) country ___countries___   (d) loaf ___loaves___

15. Add punctuation marks as needed in the sentence below.
(80, 88)

"In what state are the Carlsbad Caverns?" asked Ernesto.

16. Circle the coordinating conjunction in the compound sentence below.
(75)

The cave is dark, (but) I have a flashlight.

17. Circle the subordinating conjunction in the sentence below.
(73)

(Since) the underground chambers are accessible, many tourists visit Carlsbad Caverns.

18. Circle the antecedent of the italicized pronoun in the sentence below.
(62)

The (bat) hangs by *its* toes and thumbs from the cave's ceiling.

19. Complete the four principal parts of the verb *swim*.
(87)

<u>*swim*</u>   <u>*(is)* swimming</u>   <u>swam</u>   <u>*(has)* swum</u>

(1) present tense   (2) present participle   (3) past tense   (4) past participle

20. Add suffixes. (2 points for each correct answer)
(33, 34)

(a) scare + y <u> scary </u>   (b) run + er <u> runner </u>

21. Underline the words that should be italicized in the sentence below.
(84)

<u>Chiroptera</u> is the scientific name for bat.

22. Circle the predicate nominative in the sentence below.
(51)

The bat is a (mammal)

23. Circle the indirect object in the sentence below.
(46, 69)

I mailed (them) a postcard from New Mexico.

On the lines provided, diagram each word of sentences 24 and 25.

24. Is this cave a home for bats?
(45, 54)

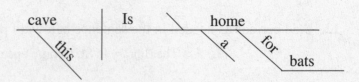

25. Huey and Lucy gave me a box of pencils.
(40, 71)

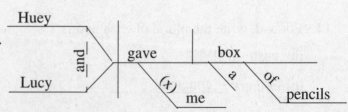

Circle the correct word(s) to complete sentences 1–10.

1. I don't have (no, any) homework today.
(93)

2. We have less homework than (they, them).
(78)

3. The pronoun *them* is (nominative, objective, possessive) case.
(70, 72)

4. The clause below is (dependent, independent):
(73)
> while they were imprisoned on Alcatraz Island

5. One of the ships (has, have) sunk.
(91)

6. (It's, Its) hunting for (it's, its) prey.
(72)

7. This box of pencils (is, are) mine.
(90)

8. The sentence below is (simple, compound):
(75)
> The ship sank, so we took a helicopter.

9. (Them, Those) ruins must be the old prison.
(82)

10. Either the horses or the cow (eat, eats) that hay.
(89)

11. For a–d, circle the correct definition. (1 point for each correct answer)

(a) Paltry means (significant, insignificant, huge).
(95)

(b) To (ostracize, languish, coerce) is to exclude from a group.
(94)

(c) Concise means (long, wordy, brief).
(92)

(d) Obfuscation is (confusion, truth, force).
(91)

12. Add periods as needed in the sentence below. (5 periods)
(47, 50)
> Dr. Parden, D.D.S., examined my teeth.

13. Circle each letter that should be capitalized in the sentence below.
(42, 43)
> alcatraz island lies in the middle of san francisco bay.

14. For a–d, write the plural of each noun.
(16, 22)

(a) ranch ___ranches___   (b) bay ___bays___

(c) city ___cities___   (d) leaf ___leaves___

15. Add punctuation marks as needed in the sentence below.
(88, 94)

"How did thirty-four prisoners escape?" asked Amelia.

16. Circle the coordinating conjunction in the compound sentence below.
(75)

We must hurry, (for) the sun is setting.

17. Circle the subordinating conjunction in the sentence below.
(73)

(Although) the island is small, it held many dangerous prisoners.

18. Add quotation marks as needed in the sentence below.
(81)

When I was a child, I sang "London Bridge Is Falling Down."

19. Complete the four principal parts of the verb *write*.
(87)

write   *(is)* writing   wrote   *(has)* written

(1) present tense   (2) present participle   (3) past tense   (4) past participle

20. Add suffixes. (2 points for each correct answer)
(33, 34)

(a) beauty + ful ___beautiful___   (b) smile + ing ___smiling___

21. Underline the words that should be italicized in the sentence below.
(84)

The artist George Henry Broughton painted Pilgrims Going to Church.

22. Circle the adverb in the sentence below.
(95)

The painter worked (tirelessly)

23. Circle the interrogative pronoun in the sentence below.
(79)

(Who) lived on Alcatraz Island before the prison was built?

On the lines provided, diagram each word of sentences 24 and 25.

24. Is this island an attraction for tourists?
(45, 54)

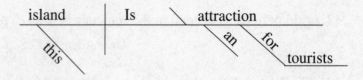

25. Can Joe or Moe pour me a cup of milk?
(40, 71)

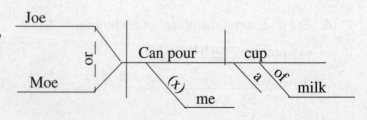

Give after Lesson 105

Circle the correct word(s) to complete sentences 1–10.

1. Polly doesn't want (no, (any)) crackers.
(93)

2. Kyle is as sagacious as (him, (he)).
(78)

3. Lucy skates (good, (well)).
(96)

4. The clause below is (dependent, (independent)):
(73)
> they live in the desert

5. One of the peacocks ((has), have) flown away.
(91)

6. Ms. Hoo and (us, (we)) shall visit the art museum.
(66)

7. The lens on this camera ((is), are) dirty.
(92)

8. The sentence below is ((simple), compound):
(75)
> A peacock flew over the fence and landed on our car.

9. (Them, (Those)) canyons have rocky cliffs.
(82)

10. Neither the peacocks nor the goose (want, (wants)) my sandwich.
(89)

11. For a–d, circle the correct definition. (1 point for each correct answer)

(a) (Profusion, (Perjury), Propriety) is lying under oath.
(96)

(b) (Profusion, Propriety, (Plagiarism)) is idea theft.
(97)

(c) Profuse means (scarce, (abundant), insignificant).
(98)

(d) A prologue comes at the ((beginning), middle, end).
(99)

12. Add periods as needed in the sentence below. (4 periods)
(47, 50)
> Dr. Jacob B. Adan rushed to St. Vincent Hospital.

13. Circle each letter that should be capitalized in the sentence below.
(42, 43)
> (c)atalina (i)sland lies off the coast of (s)outhern (c)alifornia.

14. For a–d, write the plural of each noun.
(16, 22)

(a) patch ___patches___   (b) Tuesday ___Tuesdays___

(c) county ___counties___   (d) knife ___knives___

15. Add punctuation marks as needed in the sentence below.
(88, 94)

"Ms Hoo, have you read my essay?" asked Perlina.

16. Circle the coordinating conjunction in the compound sentence below.
(75)

The sun has set, (yet) the air remains warm.

17. Add a hyphen as needed in the sentence below.
(97)

We cyclists are looking forward to our fifty-mile ride.

18. Add quotation marks as needed in the sentence below.
(81)

Is the nursery rhyme "Humpty Dumpty" about an egg?

19. Complete the four principal parts of the verb *eat*.
(87)

eat	*(is)* eating	ate	*(has)* eaten
(1) present tense	(2) present participle	(3) past tense	(4) past participle

20. Circle the word below that is divided correctly.
(99)

(un-known)   unkno-wn   unkn-own

21. Underline the words that should be italicized in the sentence below.
(84)

<u>Crotalus atrox</u> and <u>Crotalus ruber</u> are types of rattlesnakes.

22. Circle the adverb in the sentence below.
(98)

Careless painters dripped blue and yellow paint (everywhere)

23. Circle the interrogative pronoun in the sentence below.
(79)

(What) is your favorite sport?

On the lines provided, diagram each word of sentences 24 and 25.

24. Is Jill the girl with long hair?
(45, 54)

25. Joe politely offers Moe one of his mints.
(40, 71)

Circle the correct word(s) to complete sentences 1–10.

1. Polly doesn't want (nothing, **anything**) to eat.
(93)

2. Mr. Cuxil, (**who**, whom) teaches English, also coaches basketball.
(77)

3. Juan plays chess (good, **well**).
(96)

4. The clause below is (**dependent**, independent):
(73)

           until the cows come home

5. Each of the artists (have, **has**) (their, **his or her**) own style.
(91)

6. Please come with Daisy and (I, **me**).
(66, 69)

7. (Is, **Are**) your scissors sharp?
(92)

8. The sentence below is (simple, **compound**):
(75)

           The pianist played well, but the singer's voice was flat.

9. The Grand Canyon is (sure, **surely**) beautiful.
(104)

10. Of the two hikers, Jill climbs the hill (**faster**, fastest).
(102)

11. For a–d, circle the correct definition. (1 point for each correct answer)

     (a) An (anarchy, **enigma**, estuary) is a riddle or mystery.
(101)

     (b) Candid means (**honest**, dishonest, unethical).
(102)

     (c) Parsimonious means (**stingy**, generous, extravagant).
(104)

     (d) To (consecrate, **desecrate**, ameliorate) is to destroy.
(105)

12. Add periods as needed in the sentence below. (4 periods)
(47, 50)

           Ms. Hoo left at two p.m. on the last day of school.

13. Circle each letter that should be capitalized in the sentence below.
(42, 43)

           The **C**olorado **R**iver has carved the magnificent **G**rand **C**anyon in **A**rizona.

14. For a–d, write the plural of each noun.
(16, 22)

     (a) coach __coaches__   (b) library __libraries__

     (c) gallon of milk __gallons of milk__   (d) mouse __mice__

15. Add punctuation marks as needed in the sentence below.
(94, 97)

"Do the sweet-smelling flowers attract bees?" asks Andrew.

16. Add a semicolon as needed in the sentence below.
(103)

Adventuresome folk can stay at Phantom Ranch in Grand Canyon; however, it is only accessible by foot or mule.

17. Add a colon as needed in the sentence below.
(105)

The supply list includes these items: tent, sleeping bag, lantern, and canteen.

18. Add quotation marks as needed in the sentence below.
(81)

Luis wrote a poem titled "A Parsimonious Monarch."

19. Complete the four principal parts of the verb *forgive*.
(87)

forgive	*(is)* forgiving	forgave	*(has)* forgiven
(1) present tense	(2) present participle	(3) past tense	(4) past participle

20. Circle the appositive phrase in the sentence below.
(58)

Amy baked a healthful snack, whole-grain muffins with raisins.

21. Underline the word that should be italicized in the sentence below.
(84)

I think that sentence contains a superfluous and.

22. Circle the adverb in the sentence below.
(100)

The forces of erosion are constantly changing the Grand Canyon's appearance.

23. Circle the subordinating conjunction in the sentence below.
(73, 74)

I shall hike up that mountain even though I am weary.

In the boxes provided, diagram each word of sentences 24 and 25.

24. Is the orca the whale with the triangular fin?
(45, 54)

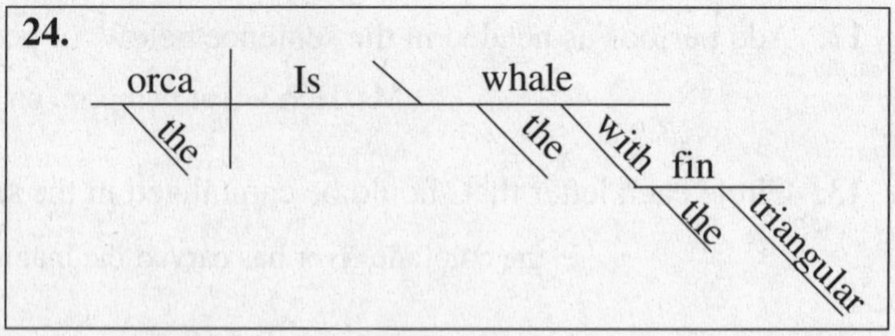

25. Has the whale swum away?
(71, 91)

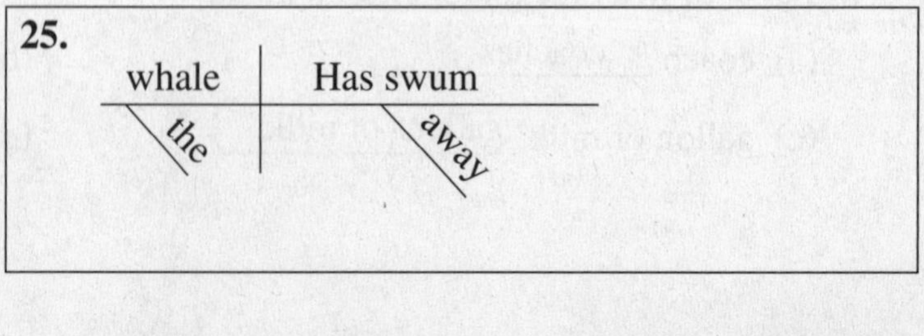

Give after Lesson 112

Circle the correct word(s) to complete sentences 1–10.

1. There wasn't (anybody, nobody) home.
(93)

2. Mr. Cuxil, (who, whom) we chose as our leader, has taught me valuable lessons.
(77)

3. Yesterday I was ill, but today I feel (good, well).
(96)

4. The clause below is (dependent, independent):
(73)
> armadillos usually live alone

5. Each of the hikers (carry, carries) (their, his or her) own food and water.
(91)

6. Please tell Elle and (I, me) your secret.
(66, 69)

7. Mumps (is, are) a miserable disease.
(92)

8. The sentence below is (compound, complex, compound-complex):
(75, 110)
> When my dog eats too much, his eyes bulge, and his stomach protrudes.

9. Josie was (real, really) frightened when she encountered a black bear.
(104)

10. (Between, Among) the many icebergs swam penguins and polar bears.
(107)

11. For a–d, circle the correct definition. (1 point for each correct answer)

(a) To (consecrate, ameliorate, beguile) is to mislead or deceive.
(106)

(b) To (beguile, digress, consecrate) is to depart from the main subject.
(107)

(c) Futile means (hopeless, effective, hopeful).
(108)

(d) (Dissension, Apathy, Digression) is lack of interest or concern.
(110)

12. Add periods as needed in the sentence below. (4 periods)
(47, 50)
> Mr. Cabrera wakes at six a.m. to exercise.

13. Circle each letter that should be capitalized in the sentence below.
(42, 43)
> can you drive from olympia, washington, to juneau, alaska?

14. For a–d, write the plural of each noun.
(16, 22)

(a) toothbrush __toothbrushes__   (b) dictionary __dictionaries__

(c) class president __class presidents__   (d) tooth __teeth__

15. Add punctuation marks as needed in the sentence below.
(88)

"Are the grizzlies hibernating?" asks Amelia.

16. Add a semicolon and a comma as needed in the sentence below.
(103)

Most states have few grizzly bears; however, Alaska has many.

17. Add a colon as needed in the sentence below.
(105)

I remember one fact about grizzlies: they are dangerous.

18. Add apostrophes as needed in the sentence below.
(108, 109)

That plumber's license wasn't valid, for it dated back to the year '73.

19. Complete the four principal parts of the verb *weave*.
(87)

weave	*(is)* weaving	wove	*(has)* woven
(1) present tense	(2) present participle	(3) past tense	(4) past participle

20. Circle the indirect object in the sentence below.
(69)

Elle offered (us) a healthful snack of nuts and fruit.

21. Underline the word that should be italicized in the sentence below.
(84)

Squash can be either a noun or a verb.

22. Circle the adverb in the sentence below.
(95)

Two black bears are (happily) feasting on wild berries.

23. Circle the subordinating conjunction in the sentence below.
(73, 74)

My dog barks (whenever) she sees a bear.

In the boxes provided, diagram each word of sentences 24 and 25.

24. Is Fifi the poodle with the red
(45, 54) collar?

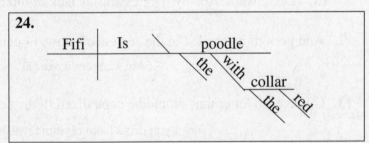

24.

25. Grizzlies can run incredibly fast.
(91, 101)

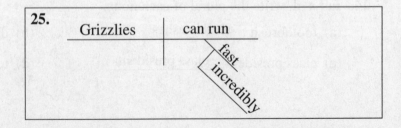

25.

More Practice Lesson 4

Circle the simple subject and underline the simple predicate in each sentence.

1. The (Earth) turns.

2. The (Sun) shines all the time.

3. (We) see it during the daytime.

4. Does the (Sun) sleep at night?

5. Can (animals) live without sunlight?

6. Can (plants) live without sunlight?

7. (We) need the Sun's light and warmth.

8. Dark (clouds) were covering the city.

9. The (Sun) had disappeared.

10. Down came the (rain).

11. (Thunder) rumbled in the distance.

12. (Fido) splashed through the puddles.

13. Do (you) have an umbrella?

14. The (rain) has stopped.

15. Out came the (Sun).

16. My tomato (plants) are growing!

17. The (seeds) have sprouted.

18. Have (you) planted a garden?

19. Soon (we) shall pick some zucchini.

20. Does (Fido) like zucchini?

Circle each letter that should be capitalized in the sentences below.

1. my friend kelly crossed the famous golden gate bridge in san francisco, california.   8 capital letters

2. the panama canal connects the pacific ocean and the caribbean sea.   7 capital letters

3. the amazon river in south america flows into the atlantic ocean.   7 capital letters

4. i think niagara falls, between lake erie and lake ontario, is spectacular!   7 capital letters

5. you will find the andes mountains in south america.   5 capital letters

6. in the center of canada lies lake winnipeg.   4 capital letters

7. phil hopes to sing the famous hymn "amazing grace" at carnegie hall in new york city next april.   9 capital letters

8. last wednesday, i read the poem "trees" by joyce kilmer.   6 capital letters

9. mr. gallup teaches at pasadena city college in california.   6 capital letters

10. is concord the capital of new hampshire?   4 capital letters

11. have you ever swum in the mediterranean sea?   3 capital letters

12. monty and allison surf in the pacific ocean.   4 capital letters

13. yes, boston is the capital of massachusetts.   3 capital letters

14. the *titanic*, a luxury ship from great britain, hit an iceberg off the coast of newfoundland.   5 capital letters

15. last july the rivas family camped near the grand canyon in arizona.   7 capital letters

Circle each helping verb in the following sentences.

1. Long ago, Alabama (was) called the Cotton State.

2. People (may) see moose, elk, caribou, and bears in Alaska.

3. Someday I (shall) visit the Grand Canyon in Arizona.

4. We (might) search for diamonds in Arkansas!

5. Gold (was) found in California in 1848.

6. Next winter Brent (will) (be) skiing in Colorado.

7. The Connecticut Colony (had) written a constitution more than a hundred years before the War of Independence.

8. (Do) people still live in Delaware's colonial homes?

9. In Florida's Everglades, a crocodile (is) sleeping peacefully.

10. Former President Jimmy Carter (was) born in Georgia.

11. (Did) this pineapple come from Hawaii?

12. (Do) all potatoes come from Idaho?

13. Our plane (will) land at O'Hare Airport in Chicago, Illinois, at 7:30 p.m.

14. (Does) Indiana manufacture baseball bats?

15. Nathan (has) (been) packing popcorn in Iowa for thirty years.

16. (Have) you driven through the wheat fields of Kansas?

17. Buffalo (were) wandering through the Kentucky mountains.

18. The Mississippi Delta (has) provided rich farmland in Louisiana.

19. People in Maine (have) built many ships.

20. (Did) your ship sail into the Chesapeake Bay in Maryland?

The Fund Raiser

Teacher instructions:

(1) Have students number blank, lined papers from 1 to 22. Ask them to write an example of the part of speech indicated beside each number. Proceed slowly, making sure students have written correct examples.

(2) Give each student a copy of the story. Ask students to write each word from their list into the blank with the corresponding number.

(3) Ask some students to read their stories aloud.

Three clever friends, (1) _____, (2) _____,
          proper noun (person)   proper noun (person)

and (3) _____, wanted to raise money to purchase
       proper noun (person)

more (4) _____ for (5) _____. Their plan was to
        concrete plural noun   proper noun (place)

manufacture (6) _____ from (7) _____ and sell
               concrete plural noun   concrete plural noun

them to (8) _____, (9) _____, and others who
          proper noun (person)   proper noun (person)

might be interested.

In preparation for the project, the three clever friends

(10) _____ and (11) _____ for many hours.
     past tense action verb   past tense action verb

United in their efforts, they were truly a (12) _____.
                                                collective noun

After working together for nearly (13) _____
                                        number

weeks, they finally had their first product to sell. It looked

like a (14) _____ but made them think of
           concrete singular noun

(15) _____ or (16) _____. Thrilled with their
     abstract singular noun   abstract singular noun

product, they felt sure that either (17) _____ or
                                          proper noun (person)

(18) _____ would buy it from them although
     proper noun (person)

(19) _____ doubted that it would sell.
     proper noun (person)

In the end the three clever friends were able to sell their

magnificent product for (20) _____ dollars to
                              number

(21) _____, who plans to rent a storage compartment
     proper noun (person)

for it in (22) _____.
              proper noun (place)

More Practice Lesson 15

Circle each letter that should be capitalized in the following sentences, poems, and song lyrics (capitalized like poems).

1. (S)tephen (F)oster wrote some humorous songs during the 1800s. (M)y friends and (I) like to sing them around the campfire.

4 capital letters

2. (I) come from (A)labama
(W)id my banjo on my knee,
(I)'m gwan to (L)ouisiana
(M)y true love for to see,
(I)t rained all night the day (I) left,
(T)he weather it was dry,
(T)he sun so hot (I) froze to death,
(S)usanna, don't you cry.

—(S)tephen (F)oster

14 capital letters

3. (M)y teacher said that (I) should stop giggling, but (I) couldn't stop because (I) was reading poems by (O)gden (N)ash. (T)hey were so funny!

7 capital letters

4. (C)elery, raw,
(D)evelops the jaw,
(B)ut celery, stewed,
(I)s more quietly chewed.

—(O)gden (N)ash

6 capital letters

5. (T)he ostrich roams the great Sahara.
(I)ts mouth is wide, its neck is narra.
(I)t has such long and lofty legs,
(I)'m glad it sits to lay its eggs.

—(O)gden (N)ash

6 capital letters

6. (W)hales have calves,
(C)ats have kittens,
(B)ears have cubs,
(B)ats have bittens,
(S)wans have cygnets,
(S)eals have puppies,
(B)ut guppies just have little guppies.

—(O)gden (N)ash

9 capital letters

Circle each letter that should be capitalized in the following titles.

1. "(d)own in the (v)alley" 2 capital letters

2. "(a) (b)icycle (b)uilt for (t)wo" 4 capital letters

3. "(i)n the (g)ood (o)ld (s)ummertime" 4 capital letters

4. "(t)he (m)an on the (f)lying (t)rapeze" 4 capital letters

5. "(t)he (s)tars and (s)tripes (f)orever" 4 capital letters

6. *(t)he (i)ndian in the (c)upboard* 3 capital letters

7. *(t)he (h)ouse at (p)ooh (c)orner* 4 capital letters

8. *(t)he (v)oyages of (d)r. (d)oolittle* 4 capital letters

9. *(t)he (l)ion, the (w)itch, and the (w)ardrobe* 4 capital letters

10. *(t)he (o)nly (g)ame in (t)own* 4 capital letters

11. *(w)here the (r)ed (f)ern (g)rows* 4 capital letters

12. *(t)he (w)ind in the (w)illows* 3 capital letters

13. *(o)ld (y)eller* 2 capital letters

14. *(t)he (p)hantom (t)ollbooth* 3 capital letters

15. *(t)he (s)ign of the (b)eaver* 3 capital letters

16. *(e)mil and the (d)etectives* 2 capital letters

17. *(t)he (t)rumpet of the (s)wan* 3 capital letters

18. *(t)he (m)ouse and the (m)otorcycle* 3 capital letters

19. *(m)y (s)ide of the (m)ountain* 3 capital letters

20. *(l)ittle (h)ouse on the (p)rairie* 3 capital letters

Circle each letter that should be capitalized in the following sentences and outlines.

1. confucius said, "virtue is not left to stand alone. he who practices it will have neighbors." 3 capital letters

2. have you read *alice's adventures in wonderland* by lewis carroll? 6 capital letters

3. yesterday i read a story called "aladdin and the wonderful lamp." 5 capital letters

4. tonight i shall read "ali baba and the forty thieves." 6 capital letters

5. as anabel drove toward boston, she sang her favorite song, "my old kentucky home." 7 capital letters

6. I. the orchestra
   A. percussion and strings
   B. the brass family
   C. the woodwind family   4 capital letters

7. II. types of musical compositions
   A. the waltz
   B. the march
   C. the symphony   4 capital letters

8. benjamin franklin said, "one today is worth two tomorrows." 3 capital letters

9. he also said, "a lie stands on one leg, truth on two." 2 capital letters

10. "the ballad of the boll weevil" is an american folk song. 5 capital letters

11. in 1892, john muir, an american naturalist, wrote to the editor of a magazine, "let us do something to make the mountains glad." 5 capital letters

12. john muir wrote about the beauty of nature in a book called *the mountains of california*. 5 capital letters

13. pearl s. buck's most popular novel, *the good earth*, won the pulitzer prize. 8 capital letters

14. james thurber, an american humorist, wrote a story called "the secret life of walter mitty." 8 capital letters

Circle each letter that should be capitalized in the following sentences.

1. (i)f (g)randpa (z)amora grew up in (n)icaragua, why doesn't he speak (e)nglish with an accent?   5 capital letters

2. Yes, (c)aptain (c)heung met (m)s. (p)han aboard the ship to (i)ndia.   5 capital letters

3. (n)ext year (i) shall take classes such as (s)panish, art, geography, mathematics, and (e)nglish.   4 capital letters

4. (a)lthough (d)r. (a)dan has taught history, he has never taught (a)merican government.   4 capital letters

5. (b)efore (a)unt (c)atherine traveled to (j)apan, she studied (j)apanese.   5 capital letters

6. (y)es, (i) believe (m)om and (d)ad invited (m)r. and (m)rs. (f)ernando (c)abrera to their anniversary party in (j)une.   9 capital letters

7. (w)hile in (e)urope, (m)om took classes in art history and (f)rench.   4 capital letters

8. (y)esterday (s)ergeant (m)undy told (m)iss (l)u that he could do nothing about the flock of (c)anadian geese in her yard.   6 capital letters

9. (d)uring our two-hour social studies class, (i) noticed that even the teacher, (d)r. (d)reamer, was yawning.   4 capital letters

10. (i) promised (m)other that (i) would clean the garage on (s)aturday.   4 capital letters

11. (i) assured (f)ather that (i) would find a safe place to store his fishing pole.   3 capital letters

12. (w)hen (a)unt (t)anisha took chemistry, there were fewer than a hundred known elements.   3 capital letters

13. (d)oes (d)eputy (c)ruz always comb her hair like that?   3 capital letters

14. (n)o, (u)ncle (w)assim, (i) cannot go fishing, for (i) have to do a homework assignment for language arts.   5 capital letters

A Parade

Teacher instructions:

(1) Have students number blank, lined papers from 1 to 26. Ask them to write an example of the part of speech indicated beside each number. Proceed slowly, making sure students have written correct examples.

(2) Give each student a copy of the story. Ask students to write each word from their list into the blank with the corresponding number.

(3) Ask some students to read their stories aloud.

(1) _____ and (2) _____ are organizing a
proper noun (person)   proper noun (person)

parade to honor their (3) _____. Floats decorated with
collective noun

(4) _____ and (5) _____ to portray the parade's
concrete plural noun   concrete plural noun

theme of (6) _____ will follow (7) _____, the
abstract singular noun   proper noun (person)

grand marshall, through the streets of the city.

People from (8) _____ and as far away as
proper noun (place)

(9) _____ will gather to watch the parade. They will
proper noun (place)

see horses (10) _____ (11) _____ and
present participle   preposition
form of action verb

(12) _____ the street. Balloons will fly
preposition

(13) _____ and (14) _____ the spectators as
preposition   preposition

marching bands (15) _____, (16) _____, and
present tense   present tense
action verb   action verb

(17) _____ to the beat of (18) _____ drums and
present tense   descriptive adjective
action verb

the clash of (19) _____ cymbals.
descriptive adjective

The most (20) _____ part of the parade will be
descriptive adjective

(21) _____ bicycle (22) _____, which will
proper possessive   collective noun
noun (person)

feature (23) _____ cyclists (24) _____
adjective (number)   present participle
form of action verb

(25) _____ banners advertising (26) _____.
preposition   abstract noun

Limiting adjectives include the following:

Articles (*a, an, the*)

Demonstrative adjectives (*this, that, these, those*)

Numbers (*one, two, three*, etc.)

Possessive adjectives (*my, his, her, Bob's, Meg's*, etc.)

Indefinites (*some, many, few*, etc.)

Circle each limiting adjective that you find in the following sentences.

1. (Delaware's) capital is Dover.

2. In (the) north, (Delaware's) width narrows to (ten) miles.

3. (Jeff's) aunt works at (a) shipyard in (that) state.

4. (Her) son left (his) gloves in (my) car.

5. (Many) people live in (the) city of Wilmington.

6. Delaware has (much) industry.

7. From (the) shore I could see (several) ships in (the) bay.

8. Have (those) sailors lost (their) way?

9. (This) state wants to protect (its) beaches from pollution.

10. Have you seen (any) gulls in (your) area?

Complete the following sentence diagrams.

1. Maine's mills produce much paper.

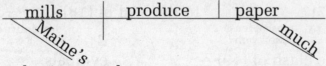

2. That business makes many computer components.

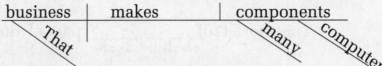

3. Maine has a cool, moist climate.

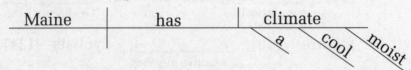

4. Two chickadees eat some seeds.

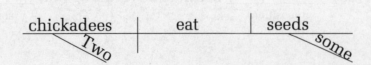

Circle each letter that should be capitalized in the following sentences.

1. (m)y grandfather worked in a (k)entucky coal mine for forty years.   2 capital letters

2. (e)very fall (i) play football with my cousins.   2 capital letters

3. (u)ncle (t)hurgood wants to tour an (a)labama auto assembly plant.   3 capital letters

4. (t)he (l)ouisiana cotton fields stretch as far as (i) can see.
3 capital letters

5. (l)ast summer (i) helped (g)randpa husk the (i)owa corn for our meal.   4 capital letters

6. (w)hen (g)eorgia peaches ripen, (a)unt (r)osa will pick a bushel.
4 capital letters

7. (h)ave you smelled the blossoms on (f)lorida orange trees?
2 capital letters

8. (m)y brother likes peanut butter, but my sister prefers (w)isconsin cheese.   2 capital letters

9. (a) (f)rench chef served mother and me a plate of steaming (c)alifornia vegetables.   3 capital letters

10. (w)ould you rather have (b)oston baked beans or (i)daho potatoes tonight?   3 capital letters

11. (m)usicians on xylophones, tambourines, and (a)frican drums created rhythms to accompany the chorus.
2 capital letters

12. (d)uring spring vacation we shall play afternoon baseball games and evening (c)hinese checkers tournaments.
2 capital letters

13. (m)ario's grandfather played a (s)teinway piano in the town's largest concert hall.   2 capital letters

14. (i) think (c)ousin (f)oster's dog is a (w)elsh terrier. 4 capital letters

15. (a) calico cat rode the muscular (g)erman shepherd with a beagle named (t)ux right behind.   3 capital letters

16. (u)ncle (b)ob planted petunias and marigolds beneath his (a)ustralian willow trees.   3 capital letters

Add periods as needed in each sentence or outline below. Then circle each period.

1. I. The state of Kansas
   A. Industry
   B. Agriculture

2. Herbert C. Hoover was the thirty-first President of the United States.

3. J. Edgar Hoover, who served as director of the Federal Bureau of Investigation, worked hard to stop organized crime.

4. Make the most of today.

5. General Robert E. Lee surrendered to General Ulysses S. Grant on April 9, 1865, in Virginia.

6. We shall read C. S. Lewis's *Chronicles of Narnia* before we see the movie.

7. I. The Southwest
   A. Arizona
   B. New Mexico
   C. Oklahoma
   D. Texas

8. Study the fifty states and their capitals.

9. Isabel M. Angles taught algebra at Francisco P. Cruz High School.

10. I. The state of Michigan
    A. History
    B. Government
    C. Economy

11. Officer U. B. Ware arrested Captain I. M. Loud for disturbing the peace.

12. Please turn down the volume.

Diagram the simple subject and simple predicate of each sentence.

1. Florida and California produce citrus fruits.

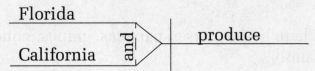

2. Mud-drenched frogs croak and leap around the pond.

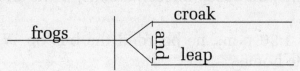

3. Elk, moose, and bison roam in Wyoming.

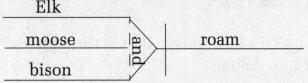

4. A coyote pauses and howls at the moon.

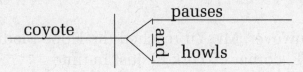

5. Maine, Vermont, and Massachusetts border New Hampshire.

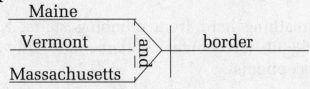

6. Amelia smiled and waved at Elle.

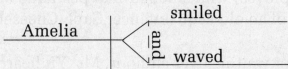

Add periods as needed. Circle each period.

1. Mr. Yu took the 10:30 a.m. bus to Farmer's Market on S. Fifth Street.

2. There he purchased bananas, grapes, potatoes, etc. for his family.

3. Altogether he spent $30.42 (thirty dollars and forty-two cents) on misc. (miscellaneous) fruits and vegetables.

4. At 1:30 p.m., he boarded the bus on W. Spring Ave. to ride home.

5. Along the bus route, a sign read, "This road closed until Thurs., Feb. 3."

6. Mr. Yu's bus moved slowly through traffic on Mt. Carmel Rd., a detour.

7. Mrs. Yu feared that her husband would be late for his 4:20 p.m. appointment with Dr. Hatchet.

8. However, Mr. Yu reached the Hope Medical Bldg. on the S.E. corner of York Pl. just in time.

9. "The gerontology dept. has moved to the seventh floor," read a sign.

10. Breathing hard from climbing stairs, Mr. Yu paid his $68.50 (sixty-eight dollars and fifty cents) to the receptionist.

11. Then he sat down next to an Antz-Be-Gone, Inc. employee, who smelled like pesticide and reminded Mr. Yu of an old acquaintance, Capt. Cheesebreath.

12. After waiting over an hour, Mr. Yu heard the receptionist say that Dr. Hatchet was performing an emergency appendectomy and would not see any more patients until 9:15 a.m. the following day.

A Field Trip

Three friends, (1)_____, (2)_____, and
proper noun (person)   proper noun (person)

(3)_____, were in charge of planning the annual class
proper noun (person)

field trip. Their goal was to plan a (4)_____ trip that
descriptive adjective

would give their classmates a sense of (5)_____. This
abstract singular noun

trip would be (6)_____ than last year's trip. In fact,
comparative adjective

this would be their (7)_____ field trip ever. It would
superlative adjective

give each classmate an opportunity to (8)_____,
present tense action verb

(9)_____, and (10)_____. The class would
present tense action verb   present tense action verb

travel (11)_____ mountains, (12)_____ tall
preposition   preposition

buildings, (13)_____ historical monuments,
preposition

(14)_____ (15)_____ rivers, and
preposition   descriptive adjective

(16)_____ the (17)_____ oceans. Besides all
preposition   descriptive adjective

this, they could photograph the many (18)_____ and
concrete plural noun

(19)_____ along the way.
concrete plural noun

Next the (20)_____ of classmates began working
collective noun

on the trip schedule. This (21)_____ journey would
descriptive adjective

begin at nine a.m. on Friday. When their teacher said that the

class would have to return by one p.m. that day for their

dictation test, the three classmates (22)_____ and
past tense action verb

frowned.

**More
Practice
Lesson 57**

Add commas as needed to the following sentences.

1. Please come to my piano recital on May 10, 2006, at the auditorium.

2. On Wednesday, September 21, 2005, I moved from my childhood home in Denver, Colorado.

3. I moved to 517 Fox Lane, Blazer Township, New Jersey 07712.

4. Blanca and Cruz visit family in Boise, Idaho, every summer.

5. Kelly drove from Salem, Oregon, to Olympia, Washington, last week.

6. Luz's new address is 4750 Long Street, Arcadia, California 91006.

7. The Southwestern states include Arizona, New Mexico, Oklahoma, and Texas.

8. Illinois, Indiana, Iowa, and Kansas are some of the Midwest states.

9. States in the Northeast include Connecticut, Delaware, Maine, Maryland, Massachusetts, and others.

10. In Alaska you can walk on a glacier, paddle a kayak, and photograph wildlife.

11. Ms. Tidbit wore a red blouse, a green skirt, a purple vest, and pink cowboy boots.

12. She carried a bag of apples, a poodle with bows in its fur, and a half-eaten sandwich.

13. Please respond to my invitation by Monday, September 19, 2005.

14. I shall show you samples of igneous, metamorphic, and sedimentary rocks.

**More
Practice
Lesson 59**

Add commas as needed to the following sentences.

1. Try, my dear cousin, to remember which goal belongs to the other team.

2. Ask me, Wakefield, if you have any questions.

3. Grandma, where were you born?

4. Don't wake that sleeping tiger, Uncle Robert!

5. Aunt Waverly, have you ever seen an anteater?

6. Anteaters don't eat aunts, my silly nephew!

7. Marsha Mellow, Ph.D., has created new software for confection manufacturers.

8. Oscar Didit, D.D., teaches religion and philosophy at the university.

9. Jaime Chavez, M.B.A., became president of a large publishing company.

10. Did Duc Eng, R.N., bandage your wounded knees?

11. Come back soon, my friend, for I'll miss you.

12. Dad, have you seen my grammar book?

13. You left it out in the rain, sweetheart.

14. I'm sorry, Dad.

15. Mrs. Vega, you might want to take Cornflower to Luis P. Bensen, D.V.M., for her puppy shots.

16. Cornflower has already had her puppy shots, Mary.

17. Did Charles B. Heale, L.P.N., care for you at the hospital?

18. I've never met him, Wassim.

Insert commas to offset the nonessential appositives in the sentences below.

1. Ogden Nash, a famous poet, wrote some hilarious limericks.

2. High-tech industries prosper in Raleigh, the capital of North Carolina.

3. I asked my best friend, Terrance, if he knew my sister's best friend, Wilda.

4. The oboe, a woodwind instrument, can sound sad.

5. *Pianissimo,* an Italian word, means "very quiet."

6. The French horn, a brass instrument, is shaped like a circle.

7. Tom plays the tuba, the largest horn in the brass family.

8. Peter Tchaikovsky, a Russian composer, wrote *The Nutcracker* and many other ballets.

9. Richmond, the capital of Virginia, has some wonderful museums and theaters.

10. The capital of Kansas, Topeka, lies west of Kansas City.

11. Gutzon Borglum, an amazing sculptor, carved four Presidents in the Mount Rushmore National Memorial in South Dakota.

12. Wisconsin, America's Dairyland, is famous for its milk and cheese.

13. Abraham Lincoln, our sixteenth President, lived in Illinois for many years.

14. Have you seen Penelope, my miniature rabbit?

15. She hasn't eaten her dinner, two juicy carrots and some alfalfa.

Add commas to offset introductory and interrupting elements and afterthoughts.

1. Without a doubt, that was the funniest story I've ever heard.

2. Max attended a ballet for the first time, I believe, last Friday night.

3. He had never seen people dance on their toes, it seems.

4. The dancers, of course, were extremely athletic.

5. Their talent, I thought, was superb!

6. Max doesn't appreciate ballet, I guess.

7. In my opinion, his comment revealed his ignorance.

8. No, he was not trying to be silly.

9. He said that they should have hired taller dancers, of all things.

10. Yes, I laughed out loud.

Underline the dependent clause in each sentence, and circle the subordinating conjunction.

1. (Although) he does not dance well, he has many other talents.

2. I have heard (that) he plays the oboe.

3. (When) she was six, she learned to swim.

4. (If) you turn left, you will come to the state Capitol building.

5. I shall not accept your money (because) bribery is unethical.

6. (While) John was elated at first, his elation did not last long.

7. An ornithologist might know (where) those eagles sleep.

8. Perhaps the meteorologist can tell us (when) the storm will hit.

9. (Though) he feigns bravery, he is frightened.

10. (If) the facts are pertinent, you may use them in your essay.

11. (Since) Eli was contrite, Ms. Hoo forgave him.

12. They call Raj a linguist (because) he speaks several languages.

Place commas where they are needed in these sentences.

1. David is a genteel, industrious landscape artist.

2. When the boss arrived, she found indolent, disrespectful employees sitting around and sipping lemonade.

3. Lulu's superfluous, bulky baggage slows her on the trip.

4. Because we had a helpful, intuitive guide, we made it safely through the dark, dangerous jungle.

5. Before you were born, an elderly, benevolent man donated land for the park.

6. As soon as you finish, we shall take a long, pleasant drive through the countryside.

7. His wild, ridiculous story was implausible.

8. If you can tolerate hot, humid weather, then you will enjoy Florida in the summer.

9. My sensible, frugal aunt washed her paper plate and cup.

10. Her wealthy, extravagant uncle threw away his fancy, costly mug because it was dirty.

11. He gave me the valuable, intangible gift of his time.

12. I had the momentary, worrisome thought that it might rain on our parade.

Place commas where they are needed in these sentences.

1. Mom told me, "Your great-grandparents' home was quaint and serene."

2. "I especially liked the potbellied stove," she said.

3. Wally shouted, "Watch out for the poison ivy!"

4. She tripped and fell, for the trail was steep and rocky.

5. Sue helped her up, and I carried her backpack.

6. That sentence goes on and on, but it is not redundant.

7. My sagacious friend studied hard, yet she forgot the capital of Alaska.

8. Molly moaned, "How could I have forgotten Juneau?"

9. Elle asked, "What is the capital of Wyoming?"

10. "I think it's Cheyenne," said Kurt.

11. Elle was not sure, so she looked at a map.

12. Elle said, "I cannot find Shy Ann on the map."

Place quotation marks where they are needed in these sentences.

1. "An ice pack might meliorate the swelling," said Dr. Lacy.

2. Juan asked, "Is the melioration of swelling important?"

3. "Swelling," said Dr. Lacy, "can cause discomfort."

4. Ms. Hoo said, "Do not let prepositions daunt you."

5. "Prepositions don't daunt me. It's the diagramming!" cried Liz.

6. "Keep trying," said Ms. Hoo, "and you will learn."

7. "I once knew a dauntless explorer," she said, "who failed again and again."

8. "Did he or she ever succeed?" asked Liz.

9. "Of course," said Ms. Hoo, "but it took a long time."

10. Liz said, "Long and complicated sentences confuse me."

11. "Besides," she added, "diagramming taxes my brain cells."

12. "Diagramming," said Ms. Hoo, "will strengthen those brain cells."

More Practice Lesson 81

In the following sentences, enclose titles of songs and short literary works in quotation marks.

1. Ivy wrote a poem called "Oh, to Be a Bird!"

2. I titled my short story "In the Nick of Time."

3. Josh Billings's essay, "The Bumblebee," made people laugh.

4. A newspaper article called "Paper Sculpture" caught my eye.

5. All the way to Des Moines, they sang "She'll be Comin' Round the Mountain."

6. Can you play "Jingle Bells" on the clarinet?

7. Professor Cruz gave a lecture titled "How to Develop Good Study Habits."

8. "Backpacking in the High Sierras" is the magazine article that sparked my interest.

9. My friend titled her expository essay "Safety Tips for Kayaking."

10. People began tapping their feet to the song "Grandma's Feather Bed."

11. Please do not sing "Found a Peanut" again!

12. Max's poem, "The Banana Slug," won first prize.

Underline all words that should be italicized in print.

1. Dad's favorite movie is <u>The Music Man</u>.

2. Quan reads <u>The Rocky Mountain News</u> every morning.

3. Have you seen the big musical production <u>Pilgrim</u>?

4. Caleb listens to a music CD called <u>White Noise</u>.

5. Someday I shall read Herman Melville's novel <u>Moby Dick</u>.

6. The aircraft carrier <u>U.S.S. Constitution</u> just left the harbor.

7. Karen named her sailboat the <u>Pelican</u>.

8. Have you seen Thomas Gainsborough's painting <u>Blue Boy</u>?

9. Max does not appreciate ballet, but he went to see <u>The Nutcracker</u> anyway.

10. Please use the word <u>subvert</u> in a sentence.

11. It's scientific name is <u>Columba fasciata</u>, but we call it a pigeon.

12. What does the Spanish word <u>demasiado</u> mean?

Complete this irregular verb chart by writing the past and past participle forms of each verb.

	VERB	PAST	PAST PARTICIPLE
1.	beat	beat	(has) beaten
2.	bite	bit	(has) bitten
3.	bring	brought	(has) brought
4.	build	built	(has) built
5.	burst	burst	(has) burst
6.	buy	bought	(has) bought
7.	catch	caught	(has) caught
8.	come	came	(has) come
9.	cost	cost	(has) cost
10.	dive	dove or dived	(has) dived
11.	drag	dragged	(has) dragged
12.	draw	drew	(has) drawn
13.	drown	drowned	(has) drowned
14.	drive	drove	(has) driven
15.	eat	ate	(has) eaten
16.	fall	fell	(has) fallen
17.	feel	felt	(has) felt
18.	fight	fought	(has) fought
19.	find	found	(has) found
20.	flee	fled	(has) fled
21.	fly	flew	(has) flown
22.	forget	forgot	(has) forgotten
23.	forgive	forgave	(has) forgiven

Circle the correct verb form for each sentence.

1. Yesterday the Jays (beated, beat) the Doves in soccer.

2. The Jays have (beat, beaten) them in every tournament.

3. For yesterday's picnic, I (brang, brought) watermelon.

4. I have always (brung, brought) watermelon.

5. Last summer we (builded, built) a treehouse.

6. We have (builded, built) two treehouses.

7. Rob (buyed, bought) a plum tree.

8. He has (buyed, bought) three trees this week.

9. Len (catched, caught) a cold.

10. He has (catched, caught) a bad one.

11. Rachel (comed, came) home early.

12. She has (came, come) home to rest.

13. Last week, apples (costed, cost) 99¢ a pound.

14. They have (cost, costed) less in the past.

15. Melody (dove, dived) into the pool.

16. She has (dove, dived) in before.

17. I (drawed, drew) a happy face.

18. I have (drawed, drawn) several.

19. Leroy (drived, drove) to Kansas City.

20. He had (drove, driven) forty miles.

21. A limb (falled, fell) from the tree.

22. Limbs have (falled, fell, fallen) every year.

23. Tomcats (fighted, fought) last night.

24. They have (fighted, fought) every night this week.

25. A goose (flied, flew) by.

26. The geese have (flew, flown) south.

Complete this irregular verb chart by writing the past and past participle forms of each verb.

VERB   PAST   PAST PARTICIPLE

	Verb	Past	Past Participle
1.	get	got	(has) gotten
2.	give	gave	(has) given
3.	go	went	(has) gone
4.	hang (execute)	hanged	(has) hanged
5.	hang (suspend)	hung	(has) hung
6.	hide	hid	(has) hidden or hid
7.	hold	held	(has) held
8.	keep	kept	(has) kept
9.	lay (place)	laid	(has) laid
10.	lead	led	(has) led
11.	lend	lent	(has) lent
12.	lie (recline)	lay	(has) lain
13.	lie (deceive)	lied	(has) lied
14.	lose	lost	(has) lost
15.	make	made	(has) made
16.	mistake	mistook	(has) mistaken
17.	put	put	(has) put
18.	ride	rode	(has) ridden
19.	rise	rose	(has) risen
20.	run	ran	(has) run
21.	see	saw	(has) seen
22.	sell	sold	(has) sold

Circle the correct verb form for each sentence.

1. The docent (gived, **gave**) a tour of the Capitol.

2. He has (gived, gave, **given**) several tours today.

3. Ana (goed, **went**) to Scotland.

4. She has (went, **gone**) once before.

5. We (hanged, **hung**) a painting on the wall.

6. We have (hanged, **hung**) paintings and photos.

7. She (hided, **hid**) the pie from me!

8. He (holded, **held**) a fluffy kitten.

9. Tom has (keeped, **kept**) the secret.

10. Pam (layed, **laid**) her pen on the table.

11. She has (layed, **laid**) two books on the table.

12. She was tired, so she (laid, **lay**) on the sofa.

13. She has (laid, **lain**) there all afternoon!

14. George (losed, **lost**) his keys again.

15. He has (losed, **lost**) them twice before.

16. I (maked, **made**) a friend yesterday.

17. I have (maked, **made**) many friends.

18. Last night, I (putted, **put**) hand lotion on my toothbrush!

19. I have never before (putted, **put**) hand lotion on anything but my hands.

20. The sun (rised, **rose**) at 6 a.m.

21. It has (**risen**, rosen) earlier each morning.

22. I (seen, **saw**) him earlier.

23. I have (**seen**, saw) him every day.

24. She (selled, **sold**) her skates.

25. She has (selled, **sold**) two pairs of skates.

Complete this irregular verb chart by writing the past and past participle forms of each verb.

VERB	PAST	PAST PARTICIPLE
1. set	set	(has) set
2. shake	shook	(has) shaken
3. shine (light)	shone	(has) shone
4. shine (polish)	shined	(has) shined
5. shut	shut	(has) shut
6. sit	sat	(has) sat
7. slay	slew	(has) slain
8. sleep	slept	(has) slept
9. spring	sprang, sprung	(has) sprung
10. stand	stood	(has) stood
11. strive	strove	(has) striven
12. swim	swam	(has) swum
13. swing	swung	(has) swung
14. take	took	(has) taken
15. teach	taught	(has) taught
16. tell	told	(has) told
17. think	thought	(has) thought
18. wake	woke	(has) woken
19. weave	wove	(has) woven
20. wring	wrung	(has) wrung
21. write	wrote	(has) written

Circle the correct verb form for each sentence.

1. Lulu (setted, set) the alarm.

2. She has (setted, set) it every night.

3. He (shook, shaked) her hand.

4. She has (shaked, shaken) many hands.

5. A light (shined, shone) through the window.

6. The light has (shined, shone) each evening.

7. Josh (shined, shone) his black shoes.

8. He has (shined, shone) several pairs of shoes.

9. Jan (shutted, shut) the window.

10. She has (shutted, shut) all the windows.

11. He (sitted, sat) on the bench.

12. He has (sitted, sat) there for two innings.

13. I (slept, sleeped) twelve hours.

14. Have you ever (slept, sleeped) that long?

15. She (standed, stood) in line.

16. She has (standed, stood) there before.

17. We (swam, swum) in the pool.

18. We have (swam, swum) many laps.

19. He (taked, took) his boa to the vet.

20. He has (took, taken) it to the vet twice this week.

21. Ilbea (teached, taught) me to sew.

22. She has (teached, taught) me many new skills.

23. Grace (telled, told) me a joke.

24. Has she (telled, told) you the joke?

25. I (thinked, thought) you were sagacious.

26. I have always (thinked, thought) that.

Circle each adverb in these sentences.

1. (Yesterday) the wind blew (hard).

2. I felt (somewhat) grumpy, for it (rudely) destroyed my hairdo.

3. I have (never) heard a noise (so) loud.

4. It swept (away) my homework.

5. (Then) it stopped.

6. I had (not) (quite) finished my math.

7. I (desperately) gathered the papers (together).

8. Will the wind blow (again) (tomorrow)?

9. (Now) it has calmed (nicely).

10. Will I (ever) find all those papers?

11. I shall smooth my hair (later).

12. I (really) think my homework has disappeared (forever).

Replace commas with semicolons where they are needed in these sentences.

1. We shall pass through Denver, Colorado; Austin, Texas; and Memphis, Tennessee.

2. He plays the piano; she plays the drums, the flute, and the trumpet.

3. Carrots, celery, and peas are vegetables; apples, oranges, and bananas are fruits.

4. They have ants in their kitchen; moreover, termites are eating the door frame.

5. George washed the car, cleaned the house, and mowed the lawn; consequently, he fell asleep during the movie.

6. It snowed; therefore, I wore a jacket.

7. Gia and Allison will be there; also, Cecilia will come if she can.

8. Mae enjoys planting trees; for example, she planted two pines and an oak today.

9. Rita cleaned the garage; furthermore, she organized all the tools and boxes.

10. The sky was cloudy; nevertheless, we went to the park.

11. Ms. Hoo wore high heels; as a result, her feet hurt.

12. Would you rather visit Richmond, Virginia; Juneau, Alaska; or Phoenix, Arizona?

Insert apostrophes where they are needed in these sentences.

1. She couldn't remember whether she'd been in Mexico in '88 or '89.

2. Mr. Collins yelled, "Good mornin'!" to his neighbor.

3. "Oh my," exclaimed Mabel, "They were just walkin' and talkin', and they never saw the bus leavin'!"

4. Can't you see that I haven't time to waste?

5. Didn't Mom graduate from high school with the class of '80?

6. Isn't her frugality obvious?

7. We're going to the library. Aren't you?

8. They're going to the library also.

9. Wouldn't you like to join us?

10. She'll come if she can.

11. We'll forgive her if she doesn't come.

12. We couldn't see through the foggy window.

Circle the correct word(s) to complete sentences 1–5.

1. A (subject, (sentence)) is a word group that expresses a complete thought.
(1)

2. The two essential parts of a sentence are the subject and the (predator, (predicate)).
(1)

3. The ((subject), predicate) tells whom or what the sentence is about.
(1)

4. The (subject, (predicate)) tells what the subject does, is, or is like.
(1)

5. A complete sentence has ((two), four) main parts.
(1)

6. For a–e, circle the correct definition. (1 point for each correct answer)

(a) Essential means (opposite, (necessary), unnecessary).
(1)

(b) Antonyms are (dinosaurs, (opposites), optimists).
(2)

(c) Abundant means (scarce, (plentiful), essential).
(3)

(d) Pessimism is the belief that things are going to get (better, (worse)).
(4)

(e) *Their* and *there* are (synonyms, antonyms, (homophones)).
(5)

For 7–10, write whether the sentence is declarative, interrogative, exclamatory, or imperative.

7. Rosa Parks refused to give up her seat in a bus. ___declarative___
(2)

8. How cold does it get in Alaska? ___interrogative___
(2)

9. Bring water on your hike through the desert. ___imperative___
(2)

10. It's a rattlesnake! ___exclamatory___
(2)

Circle the simple subject of sentences 11–13.

11. Some (people) in Arkansas listen to delightful kitchen bands.
(3)

12. Can (Jenny) play the fiddle?
(3)

13. (Archaeologists) have found dinosaur fossils in Colorado.
(3)

Circle the simple predicate of sentences 14–16.

14. Some people in Arkansas (listen) to delightful kitchen bands.
(4)

16. Archaeologists have found dinosaur fossils in Colorado.
(4)

For 17–19, write whether the word group is a sentence fragment or a complete sentence.

17. Picking seeds from the watermelon. _____
(5)

18. Mount McKinley is the tallest mountain in North America. _____
(5)

19. To catch a catfish in the pond. _____
(5)

20. Draw a vertical line between the subject and predicate parts of the sentence below.
(1)

Horseshoe crabs have endured the changes of man.

Circle the correct word(s) to complete sentences 1–5.

1. Yesterday Martin (fry, fries, fried) catfish for supper.
(10)

2. An alligator (sleep, sleeps) in the Everglades.
(9)

3. Leon (ski, skis) in Vail, Colorado.
(9)

4. The sentence below is (declarative, interrogative, exclamatory, imperative).
(2)

Look at all the ladybugs!

5. The sentence below is (declarative, interrogative, exclamatory, imperative).
(2)

Use sunscreen at the beach.

6. For a–e, circle the correct definition. (1 point for each correct answer)

(a) (Its, It's) is the possessive form of *it*.
(6)

(b) To disclose is to (hide, uncover, sneeze).
(7)

(c) (Geology, Archipelago, Flora) is earth science.
(8)

(d) An archipelago is a chain of many (beads, islands, events).
(9)

(e) Fauna is (plant, animal) life.
(10)

7. On the lines below, make a complete sentence from the following sentence fragment:
(6)

After finishing this test, _____

_____

Circle the action verb in sentences 8 and 9.

8. Various space missions launch from Cape Canaveral.
(7)

9. Groups protect endangered species such as whales.
(7)

10. In the sentence below, circle each proper noun needing a capital letter.
(8)

ruth handler created plastic dolls named barbie in denver, colorado.

Circle the simple subject of sentences 11–13.

11. Skiers flock to the snow-capped mountains of Colorado.
(3)

12. Are students at the university working hard?
(3)

13. Here is a famous seafood restaurant.
(3)

Circle the simple predicate of sentences 14–16.

14. Skiers flock to the snow-capped mountains of Colorado.
(4)

15. Students at the university are working hard.
(4)

16. Here is a famous seafood restaurant.
(4)

For 17–19, write whether the word group is a sentence fragment or a complete sentence.

17. Jimmy Carter, our thirty-ninth President ,was born in Georgia. _____
(5)

18. To begin selling peanut butter. _____
(5)

19. Measuring the enormous span of the pelican's wings. _____
(5)

20. Draw a vertical line between the subject and predicate parts of the sentence below.
(1)

The 1858 Gold Rush began in Colorado at Pike's Peak.

Circle the correct word(s) to complete sentences 1–5.

1. The two essential parts of a sentence are the (subordinate, subject) and the predicate.
(1)

2. The simple (subject, predicate) is the main word or words in a sentence that tell who or what is doing or being something.
(3)

3. Norma (carve, carves) ice sculptures in Minnesota.
(9)

4. The sentence below is (declarative, interrogative, exclamatory, imperative).
(2)

Does Michigan have copper mines?

5. The sentence below is a (complete sentence, sentence fragment).
(5)

Named for the Indian word meaning great lake.

6. For a–e, circle the correct definition. (1 point for each correct answer)

(a) An isthmus is a narrow strip of (land, ocean, water) connecting two larger bodies of land.
(11)

(b) A (lagoon, strait, peninsula) is a narrow waterway connecting two larger bodies of water.
(12)

(c) A (delta, tributary, archipelago) is a river or stream that flows into a larger river or stream.
(13)

(d) A (strait, lagoon, hemisphere) is one half of the earth.
(14)

(e) (Meridian, Hemisphere, Latitude) is a distance north or south of the equator.
(15)

7. On the lines below, rewrite and correct the sentence fragment, making a complete sentence.
(6)

Fur traders trapping wolverines.

_____

_____

8. Circle the action verb in the sentence below.
(7)

People nicknamed Michigan the Wolverine State.

9. In the sentence below, replace the blank with the correct verb form.
(10)

Chi (past of *shop*) _____ at the Mall of America in Bloomington, Minnesota.

10. In the sentence below, circle each proper noun needing a capital letter.
(8)

michigan's windmill island municipal park has an authentic dutch windmill.

11. Circle the simple subject in the sentence below.
(3)

Along came Melody on a calico horse.

12. Circle the simple predicate in the sentence below.
(4)

Along came Melody on a calico horse.

13. Circle the abstract noun in the following list: horse, island, pessimism, peninsula, wolverine
(11)

14. Circle the word from this list that could *not* be a helping verb: is, am, are, was, were, be, and
(12)

15. Circle the compound noun from this list: Washington, afternoon, predicate, optimism
(13)

16. Circle the possessive noun in the sentence below.
(13)

Minnesota's prairie has a large gopher population.

Circle each letter that should be capitalized in 17–19.

17. i am always amazed at how little i know.
(15)

18. a famous medical center, mayo clinic treats people from all over the world.
(15)

19.
(15)
        i love my red rooster;
        my rooster loves me.
        i love my red rooster
        under the cottonwood tree.

20. Draw a vertical line between the subject and predicate parts of the sentence below.
(1)

A statue of Paul Bunyan stands in Bemidji, Minnesota.

Circle the correct word(s) to complete sentences 1–5.

1. *John's* is a (possessive, plural) noun.
(13)

2. *Team* is a (compound, collective) noun.
(11)

3. A diamond (scratch, scratches) granite.
(9)

4. The sentence below is (declarative, interrogative, exclamatory, imperative).
(2)

Don't eat too many French fries.

5. The sentence below is a (complete sentence, sentence fragment).
(5)

To build and repair submarines.

6. For a–e, circle the correct definition. (1 point for each correct answer)

   (a) A (mesa, plateau, chasm) is a deep, wide crack in the earth's surface.
   (20)

   (b) (Arroyo, Atoll, Tundra) is a flat, frozen, treeless plain.
   (19)

   (c) Trees do not grow above the (timber, date, twenty-yard) line.
   (18)

   (d) The Tropic of Cancer is an imaginary (friend, line, atoll) parallel to the equator.
   (17)

   (e) A(n) (arroyo, atoll, savanna) is a circular coral reef.
   (16)

7. On the lines below, write the four principal parts of the verb *plant*.
(19)

    _____   (is) _____   _____   (has) _____

     (present tense)   (present participle)   (past tense)   (past participle)

8. Circle the two action verbs in the sentence below.
(7)

Today, people in New Hampshire's shipyards build and repair submarines.

9. In the sentence below, replace the blank with the correct verb form.
(10)

The sculptor (past of *chip*) _____ the granite.

10. Circle each preposition in the sentence below.
(20)

Without good sense, an explorer ventures into a dark cave.

11. Circle the simple subject in the sentence below.
(3)

On the eastern border of New Hampshire are shipyards.

12. Circle the simple predicate in the sentence below.
(4)

On the eastern border of New Hampshire are shipyards.

13. In the sentence below, replace the blank with the correct verb form.
(18)

New Hampshire (past of *be*) _____ the first to declare independence from Great Britain.

14. Circle the word from this list that is *not* a preposition: about, before, by, for, from, drown
(20)

15. For a–e, write the plural of each singular noun. (1 point for each correct answer)
(16, 17)

(a) sky _____

(b) Lewis _____

(c) eggplant _____

(d) loaf _____

(e) tooth _____

16. Circle the possessive noun in the sentence below.
(13)

Vines covered the cave's entrance.

Circle each letter that should be capitalized in 17 and 18.

17. i have never read *miss pickerell goes to mars*.
(15)

18. alejandro will climb mount washington to the highest point in new england.
(15)

19. Circle the entire verb phrase in the sentence below.
(12)

People in Portsmouth have been building ships since 1630.

20. Draw a vertical line between the subject and predicate parts of the sentence below.
(1)

Eva's great-grandfather planted potatoes in New Hampshire.

Give after Lesson 30

Circle the correct word(s) to complete sentences 1–11.

1. (Do, Did) Johnny Appleseed plant apple trees in Ohio?
(18)

2. We (will, shall) see Ohio's Rock and Roll Hall of Fame tomorrow.
(14)

3. Thomas Edison invented and (perfects, perfected) the lightbulb.
(10)

4. The sentence below is (declarative, interrogative, imperative, exclamatory):
(2)

           The first cash register came from Dayton, Ohio.

5. The following is a (sentence fragment, run-on sentence, complete sentence):
(5)

           An ancient dugout canoe was found in Ohio.

6. The word *around* is a (noun, verb, preposition).
(20)

7. The noun *lightbulb* is (abstract, concrete).
(11)

8. The noun *compass* is (singular, plural).
(13)

9. To *placate* means to (disturb, anger, calm).
(22)

10. To *ignite* is to (disclose, burn, freeze).
(25)

11. Jenny and Phil marry. Phil (marrys, marries) Jenny.
(9)

12. Write the plural form of a–d:
(16, 17)

     (a) tooth _____   (b) cuff _____   (c) county _____   (d) ditch _____

Circle each letter that should be capitalized in 13–15.

13. one sometimes reads of johnny appleseed. his trees still grow around ohio.
(15)

14. rhett butler remains a popular character from the novel *gone with the wind*.
(25)

15. lake erie forms part of the northern border of ohio.
(8)

16. Circle each preposition that you find in this sentence:
(20)

     Two of the astronauts, Neil Armstrong and John Glenn, are from the state of Ohio.

17. Circle the two helping verbs in the following sentence:
(12)

      Thomas Edison had been experimenting with electricity for many years.

18. For a–d, circle the correct irregular verb form.
(18)

    (a) She (am, is, are)   (b) They (do, does)   (c) You (has, have)   (d) He (do, does)

19. Complete the four principal parts of the verb *wish*.
(19)

      wish   *(is)* _____   _____   *(has)* _____

    (1) present tense   (2) present participle   (3) past tense   (4) past participle

20. Circle the simple subject of the sentence below.
(4)

      Deep under the ground rested the oldest watercraft.

21. Circle the simple predicate of the sentence below.
(4)

      Deep under the ground rested the oldest watercraft.

22. Write the plural form of the singular noun *commander in chief*. _____
(22)

23. Circle the action verb in the sentence below.
(7)

      The state of Ohio produces many tires.

24. Rewrite the following sentence fragment, making a complete sentence.
(6)

      To see a tire factory in Ohio.

_____

25. Rewrite and correct the run-on sentence below.
(24)

      Annie Oakley was born in Ohio she was a famous sharpshooter.

_____

Circle the correct word(s) to complete sentences 1–11.

1. (Have, Has) the museum opened yet?
(18)

2. We (will, shall) see the faces carved on Mount Rushmore.
(14)

3. Nancy went out and (talks, talked) to the horses.
(10)

4. The sentence below is (declarative, interrogative, imperative, exclamatory):
(2)

Did Wild Bill Hickock die in South Dakota?

5. The following is a (sentence fragment, run-on sentence, complete sentence):
(23)

We saw the Black Hills the trees there look almost black.

6. The word *through* is a (noun, verb, preposition).
(21)

7. The noun *peace* is (abstract, concrete).
(11)

8. The noun *cat's* is (plural, possessive).
(13)

9. A large meteorite might create a (mountain, crater, hill) on the earth's surface.
(29)

10. A(n) (meteorite, caldera, etymology) shows a word's original language and meaning.
(30)

11. Chickens scratch. A chicken (scratch, scratches).
(9)

12. Write the plural form of a–d:
(16, 17)

(a) knife _____   (b) monkey _____(c) cupful _____   (d) entry _____

Circle each letter that should be capitalized in 13–15.

13. lilah said, "that north dakota blizzard was terrible."
(26)

14. on saturday we shall read *alice in wonderland*.
(25)

15. lake ontario forms part of the northern border of new york.
(8)

16. Circle each preposition that you find in the sentence below.
(20, 21)

Since yesterday, the explorer has been inside the cave by himself, without a buddy.

17.
(12)
Circle the two helping verbs in the following sentence:

Clara Barton had been nursing the wounded for three years.

18.
(18)
For a–d, circle the correct irregular verb form.

(a) They (am, is, are)   (b) She (do, does)   (c) He (has, have)   (d) You (do, does)

19.
(19)
Complete the four principal parts of the verb *try*.

try   *(is)* _____   _____   *(has)* _____

(1) present tense   (2) present participle   (3) past tense   (4) past participle

20.
(4)
Circle the simple subject of the sentence below.

Out on the range roams a herd of buffalo.

21.
(4)
Circle the simple predicate of the sentence below.

Out on the range roams a herd of buffalo.

22.
(22)
Write the plural form of the singular noun *father-in-law*. _____

23.
(1)
Draw a vertical line between the subject and the predicate of the sentence below.

Wild Bill Hickok and Wyatt Earp chased outlaws in the Wild West.

24.
(28, 29)
Circle each silent letter in the words below.

(a) hour   (b) ridge   (c) walk   (d) debt

25.
(24)
Rewrite and correct the run-on sentence below.

South Dakota is the Mount Rushmore State its capital is Pierre.

_____

Circle the correct word(s) to complete sentences 1–10.

1. Etymologies are (antonyms, synonyms, word histories).
(30)

2. George Washington (was, were) born in Virginia.
(18)

3. Stephen stepped outide and (calls, called) his dog.
(10)

4. The sentence below is (declarative, interrogative, imperative, exclamatory):
(2)

The musical was fabulous!

5. The following is a (sentence fragment, run-on sentence, complete sentence):
(5)

Buried treasure in the Mojave Desert.

6. The word *at* is a (noun, verb, preposition).
(21)

7. The noun *backpack* is (abstract, concrete).
(11)

8. The noun *cats* is (plural, possessive).
(13)

9. The verb (look, laugh, smile) is a common linking verb.
(31)

10. Many people watch. One person (watch, watches).
(9)

11. For a–d, circle the correct definition. (1 point for each correct answer)

(a) (Kin, Clamor, Panacea) refers to one's relatives.
(35)

(b) A (kin, clamor, panacea) is a loud cry or uproar.
(34)

(c) (Clamor, Indispensable, Dispensable) means absolutely necessary.
(33)

(d) The Greek root *pan* means (fire, table, all).
(32)

12. Write the plural form of a–d:
(16, 17)

(a) suffix _____ (b) inch _____ (c) dairy _____ (d) deer _____

Circle each letter that should be capitalized in 13–15.

13. mrs. ng asked, "have you seen meg's other shoe?"
(26)

14. please read me "the cat in the hat."
(25)

15. the mississippi river forms the eastern border of arkansas.
(8)

16. Circle each preposition that you find in the sentence below.
(20, 21)

        Over this hill and across the field lies a grove of apple trees with many blossoms.

17. For a–d, circle the word that is spelled correctly. (1 point for each correct answer)
(33-35)

    (a) weigh, wiegh   (b) decieve, deceive   (c) forgeting, forgetting (d) countries, countrys

18. For a–d, circle the correct irregular verb form. (1 point for each correct answer)
(18)

    (a) He (am, is, are)   (b) I (am, is, are)   (c) She (has, have)   (d) It (do, does)

19. Complete the four principal parts of the verb *flap*.
(19)

        <u>flap</u>   *(is)* _____   _____   *(has)* _____

        (1) present tense   (2) present participle   (3) past tense   (4) past participle

20. Add suffixes. (2 points for each correct answer)
(33)

    (a) dry + est _____   (b) say + ed _____

21. Add suffixes. (2 points for each correct answer)
(34)

    (a) glad + ly _____   (b) begin + ing _____

22. From the following list, circle the word that could *not* be a linking verb: is, am, are, wash, were
(31)

23. Circle each silent letter in the words below. (1 point for each correct answer)
(28, 29)

    (a) who   (b) receipt   (c) lamb   (d) climb

On the lines provided, diagram the simple subject and simple predicate of sentences 24 and 25.

24. Across the desert gallops an Arabian horse.
(32)

25. Has the stallion seen the mare?
(32)

Circle the correct word(s) to complete sentences 1–10.

1. (Etymologies, Atolls, Peninsulas) are word histories.
(30)

2. (Do Does) she like jazz music?
(18)

3. A muddy beagle (follows, followed) me home yesterday.
(10)

4. The word group below is a (phrase, clause):
(36)

throughout the state of Washington

5. The following is a (sentence fragment, run-on sentence, complete sentence):
(23)

Nevada gets very little rain it is mostly desert.

6. The word *across* is a (noun, verb, preposition).
(20)

7. The noun *miracle* is (abstract, concrete).
(11)

8. The noun *Jameses* is (plural, possessive).
(13)

9. The verb (wait, seem, stare) is a common linking verb.
(31)

10. Sodas fizz. A soda (fizzs, fizzes).
(9)

11. For a–d, circle the correct definition. (1 point for each correct answer)

(a) A (dogmatic, timid, humble) person speaks with authority and sometimes arrogance.
(39)

(b) To humiliate is to shame or (exalt, praise, embarrass).
(38)

(c) A heavy load might (encourage, enable, encumber) a traveler.
(37)

(d) Avarice is (generosity, greed, patience).
(36)

12. Write the plural form of a–d:
(16, 17)

(a) fax _____   (b) dish _____   (c) baby _____   (d) child _____

Circle each letter that should be capitalized in 13–15.

13. addicus asked, "did you find that book on ms. blue's bookshelf?"
(26)

14. may i borrow your copy of *alice in wonderland*?
(25)

15. i offered ms. hoo some hot french bread.
(38)

16. Circle each preposition that you find in the sentence below.
(20, 21)

> Without your help, I could not have rescued my horse from the flood.

17. For a–d, circle the word that is spelled correctly. (1 point for each correct answer)
(33-35)

   (a) nieghbor, neighbor   (b) priest, preist   (c) runing, running (d) librarys, libraries

18. Circle each limiting adjective in the sentence below.
(40)

> Fernando's band has a drummer, a pianist, and two guitarists.

19. Complete the four principal parts of the verb *reply*.
(19)

      reply   *(is)* _____   _____   *(has)* _____

   (1) present tense   (2) present participle   (3) past tense   (4) past participle

20. Add suffixes. (2 points for each correct answer)
(33, 34)

   (a) win + ing _____   (b) pay + ed _____

21. Circle each descriptive adjective in the sentence below.
(39)

> Lush, colorful trees in beautiful Vermont attract appreciative spectators.

22. From the following list, circle the word that could *not* be a linking verb: seem, appear, blow, stay
(31)

23. Circle each silent letter in the words below. (1 point for each correct answer)
(28, 29)

   (a) sign   (b) honor   (c) listen   (d) limb

On the lines provided, diagram each word of sentences 24 and 25.

24. My puppy has chewed my new shoes.
(32)

25. Has that puppy chewed your new shoes?
(32)

Circle the correct word(s) to complete sentences 1–10.

1. (Field labels, Etymologies, Antonyms) are word histories showing the original language and
(30) meaning.

2. West Virginia (have, has) many coal mines.
(18)

3. Settlers followed the trail and (arrive, arrived) in West Virginia.
(10)

4. The word group below is a (phrase, clause):
(36)

because it lies in the Appalachian Mountain system

5. The following is a (sentence fragment, run-on sentence, complete sentence):
(5)

Jamestown, the first permanent English colony.

6. The word *the* is a (noun, verb, adjective, preposition).
(40)

7. The noun *success* is (abstract, concrete).
(11)

8. The noun *James's* is (plural, possessive).
(13)

9. The verb (think, sing, was) is a common linking verb.
(31)

10. Bees buzz. A bee (buzzs, buzzes).
(9)

11. For a–d, circle the correct definition. (1 point for each correct answer)

(a) (Frugal, Cognizant, Paternal) means having knowledge; aware.
(41)

(b) An imprudent decision is (frugal, unwise, wise).
(44)

(c) (Frugal, Cognizant, Paternal) means avoiding waste.
(42)

(d) (Frugal, Cognizant, Paternal) means of or like a father.
(43)

12. Write the plural form of a–d:
(16, 17)

(a) loaf _____ (b) cupful _____ (c) man _____ (d) piano _____

Circle each letter that should be capitalized in 13–15.

13. daniel explained, "west virginia was once a part of virginia."
(26)

14. "unfortunately, diseases such as measles, mumps, and chicken pox caused the deaths of many
(43) native americans," said daniel.

15. dear grandma,
(38, 41)
      have you visited the east?
          love,
          genevie

16. Circle each preposition that you find in the sentence below.
(20, 21)

West Virginia sided with the North during the Civil War.

17. Circle the misspelled word in the list below.
(33-35)

relieve, height, wiegh, eight, deceive

18. Circle each adjective in the sentence below.
(39, 40)

Prudent students will do the homework.

19. Complete the four principal parts of the verb *drop*.
(19)

<u> drop </u>   *(is)* <u>   </u>   <u>   </u>   *(has)* <u>   </u>
    (1) present tense   (2) present participle   (3) past tense   (4) past participle

20. Add suffixes. (2 points for each correct answer)
(33, 34)

    (a) clap + ing _____   (b) pretty + er _____

21. In the sentence below, underline the prepositional phrase and circle the object of the preposition.
(44)

Did she tell you the secret of her success?

22. Circle the proper adjective in the sentence below.
(42)

Jamestown was the first permanent English colony.

23. Circle each silent letter in the words below. (1 point for each correct answer)
(28, 29)

    (a) cupboard   (b) talk   (c) guess   (d) comb

On the lines provided, diagram each word of sentences 24 and 25.

24. Do you eat a variety of healthful foods?   variety
(40, 45)

25. A prudent student will do the homework.   *the*
(40)

Circle the correct word(s) to complete sentences 1–10.

1. The boldfaced word that begins a dictionary entry gives the (etymology, part of speech, spelling).
(27)

2. Terry (do, does) the homework.
(18)

3. He unlocked the treasure chest and (looks, looked) inside.
(10)

4. The word group below is a (phrase, clause):
(36)

six feet long with mossy, leathery skin, the alligator

5. The following is a (sentence fragment, run-on sentence, complete sentence):
(5, 23)

The man at the piano is Duke Ellington.

6. The word *an* is a (noun, verb, adjective, preposition).
(40)

7. The noun *alligator* is (abstract, concrete).
(11)

8. The noun *alligators* is (plural, possessive).
(13)

9. The verb (whisper, sneeze, smell) is a common linking verb.
(31)

10. Birds fly. A bird (flys, flies).
(9)

11. For a–d, circle the correct definition. (1 point for each correct answer)

(a) (Illiterate, Frugal, Benevolent) means unable to read or write.
(46)

(b) A (Plausible, Momentous, Intolerable) occasion is one of great importance.
(47)

(c) A believable story is (frugal, intolerable, plausible).
(48)

(d) Benevolent means (kind, believable, unbearable).
(50)

12. Add periods as needed: I   Washington D C
(47, 50)   A The White House
                                                 B The Capitol Building

Circle each letter that should be capitalized in 13 and 14.

13. nolan asked, "may i borrow your book about georgia?"
(26)

14. dear gavin,
(38, 41)
your grandfather owned land in the midwest and in the south.
          love,
          aunt bessie

15. Circle the linking verb in the sentence below.
(31)

That Georgian peach smells so sweet!

16. Circle each coordinating conjunction in the sentence below.
(48)

He toured the White House and the Capitol Building, but she went to the Smithsonian Museum.

17. Circle the misspelled word in the list below.
(33-35)

believe, nieghbor, weigh, niece

18. Circle each adjective in the sentence below.
(39, 40)

Two sleepy alligators lie in the hot sun.

19. Complete the four principal parts of the verb *cry*.
(19)

<u>cry</u>   *(is)* _____   _____   *(has)* _____

(1) present tense   (2) present participle   (3) past tense   (4) past participle

20. Add suffixes. (2 points for each correct answer)
(33, 34)

(a) trap + ed _____   (b) cloudy + er _____

21. In the sentence below, underline each prepositional phrase, circling the object of each preposition.
(44)

Lucas looks down the basketball court and sprints to the basket.

22. Circle the proper adjective in the sentence below.
(42)

Does Fido like Swiss cheese?

23. Circle the indirect object in the sentence below.
(46)

The benevolent couple gave stray dogs food and shelter.

On the lines provided, diagram each word of sentences 24 and 25.

24. Did the man at the piano play classical music?
(40, 45)

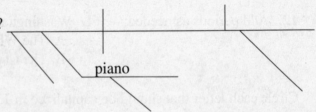

25. Joe and Moe repair and polish old bikes.
(40, 49)

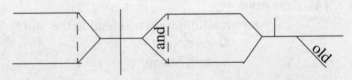

Circle the correct word(s) to complete sentences 1–10.

1. Of the two buildings, this one is (taller, tallest).
(55)

2. Terry (have, has) two brothers.
(18)

3. She closed the window and (locks, locked) the door.
(10)

4. The word group below is a (phrase, clause):
(36)

if you see an alligator with an open mouth

5. The following is a (sentence fragment, run-on sentence, complete sentence):
(5)

Duke Ellington, the man at the piano.

6. The word *the* is a (noun, verb, adjective, preposition).
(40)

7. The noun *optimism* is (abstract, concrete).
(11)

8. The noun *alligator's* is (plural, possessive).
(13)

9. The verb (honk, clap, sound) is a common linking verb.
(31)

10. Students *try* hard. A student (*trys, tries*) hard.
(9)

11. For a–d, circle the correct definition. (1 point for each correct answer)

(a) (Bovine, Canine, Feline) relates to dogs.
(51)

(b) (Bovine, Canine, Equine) relates to cows.
(52)

(c) Auditory relates to the sense of (smell, hearing, touch).
(53)

(d) Gentility is (malice, courtesy, greed).
(55)

12. Add periods as needed in the sentence below.
(47, 50)

Mr Brite wrote, "The First Ave market will be closed Tues this week"

Circle each letter that should be capitalized in 13 and 14.

13. mimi said, "some crops in the south are harvested in spring."
(26)

14. dear alsumana,
(38, 41)
do you have rollercoasters in papua, new guinea? i like fast and twisty ones.
your friend,
elisa

15. Circle the predicate nominative in the sentence below.
(51)

Mrs. Cruz is a prudent attorney.

16. Circle each coordinating conjunction in the sentence below.
(48)

Ian and Rosa are visiting North or South Carolina, but their home is in Florida.

17. Circle the misspelled word in the list below.
(33-35)

beleive, neighbor, weigh, niece

18. Circle each adjective in the sentence below.
(39, 40)

Four fuzzy rabbits hide inside a hollow log.

19. Complete the four principal parts of the verb *trap*.
(19)

<u>   trap   </u>   <u> (is)   </u>   <u>   </u>   <u> (has)   </u>

(1) present tense   (2) present participle   (3) past tense   (4) past participle

20. Add suffixes. (2 points for each correct answer)
(33, 34)

(a) cry + ed _____   (b) happy + est _____

21. In the sentence below, underline each prepositional phrase, circling the object of each preposition.
(44)

A dog with a rhinestone collar leaps into the car.

22. Circle the proper adjective in the sentence below.
(42)

Juicy California oranges make a good snack.

23. Circle the indirect object in the sentence below.
(46)

Hnin passed Borden the baton.

On the lines provided, diagram each word of sentences 24 and 25.

24. The man at the piano is my brother.
(45, 51)

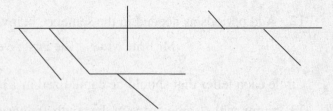

25. Joe and Moe wash and wax their car.
(40, 49)

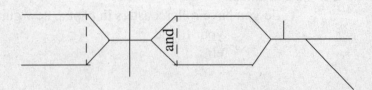

Circle the correct word(s) to complete sentences 1–10.

1. Of the two computers, this one is (better, best).
(56)

2. We (was, were) friends.
(18)

3. Yesterday he (fry, fries, fried) potatoes.
(10)

4. The word group below is a (phrase, clause):
(36)

> instead of the movie about pirates

5. The following is a (sentence fragment, run-on sentence, complete sentence):
(23, 24)

> The truck swerved it hit a curb.

6. A(n) (declarative, interrogative, imperative, exclamatory) sentence asks a question.
(2)

7. The noun *elephant* is (abstract, concrete).
(11)

8. I have two (sister-in-laws, sisters-in-law).
(13, 16)

9. The verb (touch, grab, feel) is a common linking verb.
(31)

10. Bees *buzz*. A bee (*buzzs, buzzes*).
(9)

11. For a–d, circle the correct definition. (1 point for each correct answer)

(a) (Intangible, Superfluous, Malicious) means more than needed or desired.
(58)

(b) (Opportune, Inopportune, Indolent) means suitable; well-timed.
(60)

(c) Indolent means (lazy, generous, hard-working).
(56)

(d) To illuminate is to give (food, money, light) to.
(59)

12. Add periods as needed in the sentence below.
(47, 50)

> Mrs Lynch's note reads, "Buy two lbs of apples at the Main St market"

Circle each letter that should be capitalized in 13 and 14.

13. ms. hoo said, "some states in the east are humid in summer."
(26)

14. dear rafael,
(38, 41)
> are there alligators in tallahassee, florida? i hope not.
>   your friend,
>   josef

15. Add commas as needed in the sentence below.
(57, 59)

Aunt Sue may I borrow your scissors a pen and some paper?

16. Circle each coordinating conjunction in the sentence below.
(48)

They offered soup or salad, so I chose soup.

17. Circle the misspelled word in the list below.
(33-35)

believe, neighbor, wiegh, niece

18. Circle each adjective in the sentence below.
(39, 40)

An industrious student typed sixteen long pages of notes.

19. Complete the four principal parts of the verb *fry*.
(19)

fry _____ *(is)* _____ _____ *(has)* _____
(1) present tense (2) present participle (3) past tense (4) past participle

20. Add suffixes. (2 points for each correct answer)
(33, 34)

(a) sad + est _____ (b) jolly + er _____

21. In the sentence below, underline each prepositional phrase, circling the object of each
(44) preposition.

A player in left field ducks under the ball.

22. Circle the proper adjective in the sentence below.
(42)

I sliced a shiny red Washington apple.

23. Circle the indirect object in the sentence below.
(46)

Onping bought Kim a lemonade.

On the lines provided, diagram each word of sentences 24 and 25.

24. The girl in the picture is my cousin.
(45, 51)

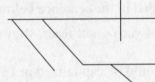

25. Joe and Moe wash and dry their dishes.
(40, 49)

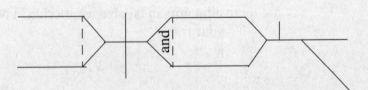

Circle the correct word(s) to complete sentences 1–10.

1. You made (less, fewer) mistakes than I did.
(56)

2. After the test, we (was, were) elated.
(18)

3. The pronoun *he* is (first, second, third) person.
(64)

4. The word group below is a (phrase, clause):
(36)

                for they produce breakfast cereal

5. The following is a (sentence fragment, run-on sentence, complete sentence):
(5, 23)

             Raising hogs in both Indiana and Illinois.

6. The hardy tree (grew, grown) quickly.
(65)

7. The noun *tenacity* is (abstract, concrete).
(11)

8. She has two (brother-in-laws, brothers-in-law).
(13, 16)

9. The verb (sing, speak, were) is a common linking verb.
(31)

10. Julia has (wore, worn) out her socks.
(65)

11. For a–d, circle the correct definition. (1 point for each correct answer)

    (a) (Gentility, Intuition, Pessimism) is an instinctive feeling or knowledge.
    (61)

    (b) Cowardice is lack of (food, money, courage).
    (62)

    (c) One who is (tenacious, malicious, indolent) does not give up.
    (63)

    (d) (Ethical, Unethical, Intrepid) means morally right.
    (64)

12. Add periods as needed in the sentence below.
(47, 50)

        Mr Cross paid $199 (one dollar and ninety-nine cents) for four lbs of bananas

13. Circle each letter that should be capitalized in the sentence below.
(42, 43)

        a british musician played the french horn skillfully.

14. For a–d, write the plural of each noun.
(16, 22)

    (a) dish _____   (b) monkey _____

    (c) baby _____   (d) spoonful _____

15. Add commas as needed in the sentence below.
(59, 60)

Ms. Hoo I would like you to meet my mother Mrs. Chavez.

16. Circle each coordinating conjunction in the sentence below.
(48)

I ordered soup and salad, for I was hungry.

17. Circle the misspelled word in the list below.
(33-35)

neighbor, weigh, view, veiw

18. Circle the antecedent of the italicized pronoun in the sentence below.
(62)

Leo left *his* skateboard outside.

19. Complete the four principal parts of the verb *wrap*.
(19)

<u>wrap</u>   *(is)* _____   _____   *(has)* _____

   (1) present tense   (2) present participle   (3) past tense   (4) past participle

20. Add suffixes. (2 points for each correct answer)
(33, 34)

(a) give + ing _____   (b) pretty + er _____

21. In the sentence below, underline each prepositional phrase, circling the object of each
(44) preposition.

The cheese on the table comes from Wisconsin.

22. Circle the proper adjective in the sentence below.
(42)

Please slice some Wisconsin cheese for sandwiches.

23. Circle the indirect object in the sentence below.
(46)

He handed me an envelope.

On the lines provided, diagram each word of sentences 24 and 25.

24. The trip was expensive but worthwhile.
(49, 54)

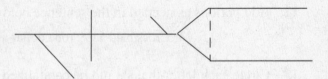

25. The little boat on the lake endured a big storm.
(40, 45)

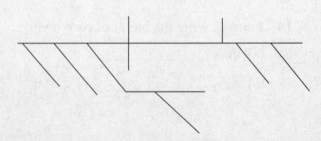

Circle the correct word(s) to complete sentences 1–10.

1. I have eaten (less, fewer) tacos than she has.
(56)

2. Doreen went to Yosemite with Austin and (I, me).
(70)

3. The pronoun *you* is (first, second, third) person.
(64)

4. The word group below is a (phrase, clause):
(36)

       a locomotive and many passenger cars at the station

5. The following is a (sentence fragment, run-on sentence, complete sentence):
(5, 23)

       The long, lonesome whistle of the steam train.

6. Vintage Shay locomotives have (blow, blew, blown) their whistles for decades.
(65)

7. The comparative form of the adjective *bad* is (bad, worse, worst).
(55, 56)

8. The word *brother-in-law's* is a (plural, possessive) noun.
(13)

9. The verb (seemed, said, whispered) is a common linking verb.
(31)

10. Julia has (drank, drunk) eight glasses of water today.
(65)

11. For a–d, circle the correct definition. (1 point for each correct answer)

     (a) Ornithology is the study of (weather, rocks, birds).
     (68)

     (b) To feign is to (pretend, listen, travel).
     (69)

     (c) (Intrepid, Tenacious, Contrite) means sorry.
     (66)

     (d) (Irrelevant, Pertinent, Contrite) means relevant or applicable.
     (67)

12. Add periods as needed in the sentence below.
(47, 50)

       At two am Ms Overwork finally finished her essay.

13. Circle each letter that should be capitalized in the sentence below.
(42, 43)

       in the east, italian americans settled to begin a new life

14. For a–d, write the plural of each noun.
(16, 22)

     (a) bench _____   (b) donkey _____

     (c) cherry _____   (d) cupful _____

15. Add commas as needed to clarify the sentence below.
(68)

With Lucy Thomas writes well.

16. Circle each coordinating conjunction in the sentence below.
(48)

I have no pen or pencil, yet I have plenty of paper.

17. Circle the misspelled word in the list below.
(33-35)

neighbor, weigh, piece, peice

18. Circle the antecedent of the italicized pronoun in the sentence below.
(62)

Sharon carries *her* heavy backpack for miles.

19. Complete the four principal parts of the verb *grow*.
(19)

<u>grow</u>   *(is)* _____   _____   *(has)* _____

(1) present tense   (2) present participle   (3) past tense   (4) past participle

20. Add suffixes. (2 points for each correct answer)
(33, 34)

(a) hope + ing _____   (b) sunny + est _____

21. In the sentence below, underline each prepositional phrase, circling the object of each
(44) preposition.

The train at the station will soon leave for Chicago.

22. Circle the proper adjective in the sentence below.
(42)

How many Georgia peaches are in this pie?

23. Circle the indirect object in the sentence below.
(46, 69)

The ranger gave us a tour of the area.

On the lines provided, diagram each word of sentences 24 and 25.

24. Your brother seems tenacious and ethical.
(49, 54)

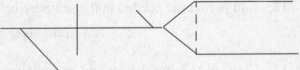

25. The rabbit in the garden ate two ripe melons.
(40, 45)

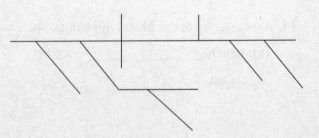

Circle the correct word(s) to complete sentences 1–10.

1. Anita is the (better, best) of the two guitarists.
(56)

2. The geology experts were Rocky and (her, she).
(66)

3. The pronoun *we* is (first, second, third) person.
(64)

4. The clause below is (dependent, independent):
(73)

when minerals form around geyser vents

5. The following is a (sentence fragment, run-on sentence, complete sentence):
(23, 24)

The geyser is quiet it will erupt soon.

6. The ship (sink, sank, sunk) long ago.
(65)

7. The superlative form of the adjective *bad* is (bad, worse, worst).
(55, 56)

8. The sentence below is (simple, compound):
(75)

The geyser blew, and I ran for cover!

9. The verb (looks, says, sings) is a common linking verb.
(31)

10. Norm has (break, broke, broken) his arm again.
(65)

11. For a–d, circle the correct definition. (1 point for each correct answer)

(a) (Serene, Ethical, Ardent) means passionate and zealous.
(71)

(b) Serene means (angry, troubled, peaceful).
(72)

(c) Sagacity is (wisdom, sorrow, trouble).
(73)

(d) (Redundancy, Linguistics, Serenity) is needless repetition.
(74)

12. Add periods as needed in the sentence below.
(47, 50)

Mrs Starlyn saw the geyser's six pm eruption

13. Circle each letter that should be capitalized in the sentence below.
(42, 43)

can i buy italian suasage in new york?

14. For a–d, write the plural of each noun.
(16, 22)

(a) lunch _____　　(b) key _____

(c) berry _____　　(d) handful _____

15. Add commas as needed in the sentence below.
(68)

When Old Faithful erupts I shall take pictures of it.

16. Circle the coordinating conjunction in the compound sentence below.
(75)

We have been watching, but the geyser has not blown.

17. Circle the misspelled word in the list below.
(33-35)

neighbor, weigh, neither, niether

18. Circle the antecedent of the italicized pronoun in the sentence below.
(62)

Although *he* has studied geology, Clark cannot explain everything.

19. Complete the four principal parts of the verb *freeze*.
(65)

freeze   *(is)* _____   _____   *(has)* _____

(1) present tense   (2) present participle   (3) past tense   (4) past participle

20. Add suffixes. (2 points for each correct answer)
(33, 34)

(a) snap + ed _____   (b) argue + ment _____

21. In the sentence below, underline each prepositional phrase, circling the object of each preposition.
(44)

A man with an umbrella stood beside me.

22. Circle the predicate nominative in the sentence below.
(51)

Old Faithful is a magnificent geyser!

23. Circle the indirect object in the sentence below.
(46, 69)

Alberto handed Quan a photo.

On the lines provided, diagram each word of sentences 24 and 25.

24. The eruption was sudden and spectacular.
(49, 54)

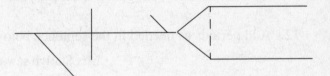

25. The man with the umbrella has two children.
(40, 45)

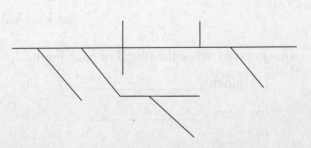

Circle the correct word(s) to complete sentences 1–10.

1. Of the two kittens, that one is (fuzzier, fuzziest).
(56)

2. You know more than (me, I) about prairie dogs.
(78)

3. The pronoun *him* is (nominative, objective, possessive) case.
(66, 69)

4. The clause below is (dependent, independent):
(73)

coyotes threaten the prairie dog colony

5. The following is a (sentence fragment, run-on sentence, complete sentence):
(5, 23)

Burrowing to escape the golden eagle.

6. A prairie dog hides in (it's, its) burrow.
(72)

7. A coyote snarls at Rocky and (he, him).
(69, 70)

8. The sentence below is (simple, compound):
(75)

The prairie dog stopped and looked at me.

9. The man (who, which) counts prairie dogs rides a horse.
(77)

10. Norm has (tear, tore, torn) his shirt again.
(65)

11. For a–d, circle the correct definition. (1 point for each correct answer)

(a) (Dauntless, Quaint, Ardent) means attractive in an old-fashioned way.
(76)

(b) To ameliorate is to (destroy, improve, harm).
(77)

(c) Dauntless means (afraid, heroic, weak).
(79)

(d) (Redundancy, Salinity, Serenity) is saltiness.
(78)

12. Add periods as needed in the sentence below.
(47, 50)

Cherries cost $299 (two dollars and ninety-nine cents) per lb, so I bought only eight oz today

13. Circle each letter that should be capitalized in the sentence below.
(42, 43)

can i purchase alaskan crab in maine?

14. For a–d, write the plural of each noun.
(16, 22)

(a) bunch _____   (b) toy _____

(c) colony _____   (d) mouthful _____

15. Add commas and quotation marks as needed in the sentence below.
(76, 80)

After lunch said Ms. Hoo we shall discuss the Utah prairie dog.

16. Circle the coordinating conjunction in the compound sentence below.
(75)

Some prairie dogs are hiding, for hawks are circling above.

17. Circle the subordinating conjunction in the sentence below.
(73)

Because prairie dogs are social animals, they live together in large colonies.

18. Circle the antecedent of the italicized pronoun in the sentence below.
(62)

Mimi likes prairie dogs because *they* are cute.

19. Complete the four principal parts of the verb *steal*.
(65)

<u>steal</u>   *(is)* _____   _____   *(has)* _____

   (1) present tense   (2) present participle   (3) past tense   (4) past participle

20. Add suffixes. (2 points for each correct answer)
(33, 34)

(a) win + er _____   (b) salty + ness _____

21. Circle the interrogative pronoun in the sentence below.
(79)

Which shall we study first?

22. Circle the predicate nominative in the sentence below.
(51)

The Utah prairie dog is an endangered species.

23. Circle the indirect object in the sentence below.
(46, 69)

Elle made Daisy a taco.

On the lines provided, diagram each word of sentences 24 and 25.

24. Prairie dogs are rodents with short tails.
(45, 54)

25. Max is listening, but Perlina is napping.
(40, 45)

Circle the correct word(s) to complete sentences 1–10.

1. That planet is the (bigger, biggest) of the two.
(56)

2. I am shorter than (he, him).
(78)

3. The pronoun *his* is (nominative, objective, possessive) case.
(70, 72)

4. The clause below is (dependent, independent):
(73)

since the moon is full tonight

5. One of the students (give, gives) (their, his or her) report each morning.
(83)

6. (Your, You're) car is fast, but (ours, our's) is faster.
(72)

7. A bear watches Grace and (she, her).
(69, 70)

8. The sentence below is (simple, compound):
(75)

The sky is cloudy, so I cannot see the stars.

9. The woman (who, which) owns the telescope can identify many stars.
(77)

10. (Them, Those) photographs show the solar eclipse.
(82)

11. For a–d, circle the correct definition. (1 point for each correct answer)

(a) A (docent, curator, culprit) is a guilty one.
(81)

(b) Bliss is great (sorrow, happiness, pain).
(82)

(c) (Subversion, Rapport, Rapprochement) is destruction.
(83)

(d) (Subversion, Rapport, Quaintness) is harmony in a relationship.
(84)

12. Add periods as needed in the sentence below.
(47, 50)

Mrs Vega lives on S First St in Denver

13. Circle each letter that should be capitalized in the sentence below.
(42, 43)

will i find washington apples in florida?

14. For a–d, write the plural of each noun.
(16, 22)

(a) branch _____   (b) day _____

(c) company _____   (d) child _____

15. Add commas and quotation marks as needed in the sentence below.
(76, 80)

Next week said Ms. Hoo we shall view a solar eclipse.

16. Circle the coordinating conjunction in the compound sentence below.
(75)

The moon is a cold, rocky body, and it has no light of its own.

17. Circle the subordinating conjunction in the sentence below.
(73)

The moon appears luminous because sunlight reflects from the moon's surface.

18. Circle the antecedent of the italicized pronoun in the sentence below.
(62)

Tex gazed at the moon until clouds covered *it*.

19. Complete the four principal parts of the verb *catch*.
(85)

<u>*catch*</u>   <u>*(is)*</u>   <u>   </u>   <u>*(has)*</u>

(1) present tense   (2) present participle   (3) past tense   (4) past participle

20. Add suffixes. (2 points for each correct answer)
(33, 34)

(a) begin + er _____   (b) happy + ness _____

21. Underline the words that should be italicized in the sentence below.
(84)

Someday I shall read Melville's novel, Moby Dick.

22. Circle the predicate nominative in the sentence below.
(51)

That solar eclipse was an awesome spectacle.

23. Circle the indirect object in the sentence below.
(46, 69)

Did Fido leave her any dog food?

On the lines provided, diagram each word of sentences 24 and 25.

24. Is Saturn the planet with rings?
(45, 54)

25. Cora and she sew their own clothes.
(40, 71)

Circle the correct word(s) to complete sentences 1–10.

1. That cave is the (bigger, biggest) of all!
(56)

2. Are you as courageous as (me, I)?
(78)

3. The pronoun *she* is (nominative, objective, possessive) case.
(70, 72)

4. The clause below is (dependent, independent):
(73)

   stalactites and stalagmites decorate the caverns

5. Each of the bats (flap, flaps) (their, its) wings.
(83)

6. (They're, Their, There) lawn is greener than (her's, hers).
(72)

7. This vase of flowers (need, needs) water.
(90)

8. The sentence below is (simple, compound):
(75)

   Inside the dark cave, bats sleep during the daytime.

9. The people (who, which) entered the cave have not come out!
(77)

10. Neither the flowers nor the lawn (have, has) been watered.
(89)

11. For a–d, circle the correct definition. (1 point for each correct answer)

   (a) Colossal means extremely (small, skinny, large).
   (86)

   (b) To (languish, daunt, coerce) is to force.
   (87)

   (c) (Colossal, Complacent, Languid) means content; self-satisfied.
   (88)

   (d) To (languish, daunt, coerce) is to grow weak.
   (89)

12. Add periods as needed in the sentence below.
(47, 50)

   That library in St George opens at nine am on Saturdays

13. Circle each letter that should be capitalized in the sentence below.
(42, 43)

   can we buy wisconsin cheese in new mexico?

14. For a–d, write the plural of each noun.
(16, 22)

   (a) bush _____   (b) valley _____

   (c) country _____   (d) loaf _____

15. Add punctuation marks as needed in the sentence below.
(80, 88)

In what state are the Carlsbad Caverns asked Ernesto

16. Circle the coordinating conjunction in the compound sentence below.
(75)

The cave is dark, but I have a flashlight.

17. Circle the subordinating conjunction in the sentence below.
(73)

Since the underground chambers are accessible, many tourists visit Carlsbad Caverns.

18. Circle the antecedent of the italicized pronoun in the sentence below.
(62)

The bat hangs by *its* toes and thumbs from the cave's ceiling.

19. Complete the four principal parts of the verb *swim*.
(87)

<u>swim</u>   <u>(is)</u>_____   _____   <u>(has)</u>_____

(1) present tense   (2) present participle   (3) past tense   (4) past participle

20. Add suffixes. (2 points for each correct answer)
(33, 34)

(a) scare + y _____   (b) run + er _____

21. Underline the words that should be italicized in the sentence below.
(84)

Chiroptera is the scientific name for bat.

22. Circle the predicate nominative in the sentence below.
(51)

The bat is a mammal.

23. Circle the indirect object in the sentence below.
(46, 69)

I mailed them a postcard from New Mexico.

On the lines provided, diagram each word of sentences 24 and 25.

24. Is this cave a home for bats?
(45, 54)

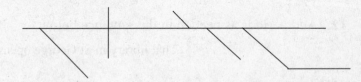

25. Huey and Lucy gave me a box of pencils.
(40, 71)

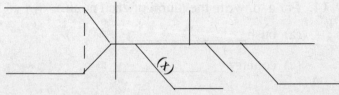

Circle the correct word(s) to complete sentences 1–10.

1. I don't have (no, any) homework today.
(93)

2. We have less homework than (they, them).
(78)

3. The pronoun *them* is (nominative, objective, possessive) case.
(70, 72)

4. The clause below is (dependent, independent):
(73)

while they were imprisoned on Alcatraz Island

5. One of the ships (has, have) sunk.
(91)

6. (It's, Its) hunting for (it's, its) prey.
(72)

7. This box of pencils (is, are) mine.
(90)

8. The sentence below is (simple, compound):
(75)

The ship sank, so we took a helicopter.

9. (Them, Those) ruins must be the old prison.
(82)

10. Either the horses or the cow (eat, eats) that hay.
(89)

11. For a–d, circle the correct definition. (1 point for each correct answer)

(a) Paltry means (significant, insignificant, huge).
(95)

(b) To (ostracize, languish, coerce) is to exclude from a group.
(94)

(c) Concise means (long, wordy, brief).
(92)

(d) Obfuscation is (confusion, truth, force).
(91)

12. Add periods as needed in the sentence below.
(47, 50)

Dr Parden, DDS, examined my teeth

13. Circle each letter that should be capitalized in the sentence below.
(42, 43)

alcatraz island lies in the middle of san francisco bay.

14. For a–d, write the plural of each noun.
(16, 22)

(a) ranch _____   (b) bay _____

(c) city _____   (d) leaf _____

15. Add punctuation marks as needed in the sentence below.
(88, 94)

How did thirty four prisoners escape asked Amelia

16. Circle the coordinating conjunction in the compound sentence below.
(75)

We must hurry, for the sun is setting.

17. Circle the subordinating conjunction in the sentence below.
(73)

Although the island is small, it held many dangerous prisoners.

18. Add quotation marks as needed in the sentence below.
(81)

When I was a child, I sang London Bridge Is Falling Down.

19. Complete the four principal parts of the verb *write*.
(87)

write   (is) _____   _____   (has) _____

(1) present tense   (2) present participle   (3) past tense   (4) past participle

20. Add suffixes. (2 points for each correct answer)
(33, 34)

(a) beauty + ful _____   (b) smile + ing _____

21. Underline the words that should be italicized in the sentence below.
(84)

The artist George Henry Broughton painted Pilgrims Going to Church.

22. Circle the adverb in the sentence below.
(95)

The painter worked tirelessly.

23. Circle the interrogative pronoun in the sentence below.
(79)

Who lived on Alcatraz Island before the prison was built?

On the lines provided, diagram each word of sentences 24 and 25.

24. Is this island an attraction for tourists?
(45, 54)

25. Can Joe or Moe pour me a cup of milk?
(40, 71)

Give after Lesson 105

Circle the correct word(s) to complete sentences 1–10.

1. Polly doesn't want (no, any) crackers.
(93)

2. Kyle is as sagacious as (him, he).
(78)

3. Lucy skates (good, well).
(96)

4. The clause below is (dependent, independent):
(73)

they live in the desert

5. One of the peacocks (has, have) flown away.
(91)

6. Ms. Hoo and (us, we) shall visit the art museum.
(66)

7. The lens on this camera (is, are) dirty.
(92)

8. The sentence below is (simple, compound):
(75)

A peacock flew over the fence and landed on our car.

9. (Them, Those) canyons have rocky cliffs.
(82)

10. Neither the peacocks nor the goose (want, wants) my sandwich.
(89)

11. For a–d, circle the correct definition. (1 point for each correct answer)

(a) (Profusion, Perjury, Propriety) is lying under oath.
(96)

(b) (Profusion, Propriety, Plagiarism) is idea theft.
(97)

(c) Profuse means (scarce, abundant, insignificant).
(98)

(d) A prologue comes at the (beginning, middle, end).
(99)

12. Add periods as needed in the sentence below.
(47, 50)

Dr Jacob B Adan rushed to St Vincent Hospital

13. Circle each letter that should be capitalized in the sentence below.
(42, 43)

catalina island lies off the coast of southern california.

14. For a–d, write the plural of each noun.
(16, 22)

(a) patch _____   (b) Tuesday _____

(c) county _____   (d) knife _____

15. Add punctuation marks as needed in the sentence below.
(88, 94)

Ms Hoo have you read my essay asked Perlina

16. Circle the coordinating conjunction in the compound sentence below.
(75)

The sun has set, yet the air remains warm.

17. Add a hyphen as needed in the sentence below.
(97)

We cyclists are looking forward to our fifty mile ride.

18. Add quotation marks as needed in the sentence below.
(81)

Is the nursery rhyme Humpty Dumpty about an egg?

19. Complete the four principal parts of the verb *eat*.
(87)

eat	*(is)* _____	_____	*(has)* _____
(1) present tense	(2) present participle	(3) past tense	(4) past participle

20. Circle the word below that is divided correctly.
(99)

un-known   unkno-wn   unkn-own

21. Underline the words that should be italicized in the sentence below.
(84)

Crotalus atrox and Crotalus ruber are types of rattlesnakes.

22. Circle the adverb in the sentence below.
(98)

Careless painters dripped blue and yellow paint everywhere.

23. Circle the interrogative pronoun in the sentence below.
(79)

What is your favorite sport?

On the lines provided, diagram each word of sentences 24 and 25.

24. Is Jill the girl with long hair?
(45, 54)

25. Joe politely offers Moe one of his mints.
(40, 71)

Circle the correct word(s) to complete sentences 1–10.

1. Polly doesn't want (nothing, anything) to eat.
(93)

2. Mr. Cuxil, (who, whom) teaches English, also coaches basketball.
(77)

3. Juan plays chess (good, well).
(96)

4. The clause below is (dependent, independent):
(73)

until the cows come home

5. Each of the artists (have, has) (their, his or her) own style.
(91)

6. Please come with Daisy and (I, me).
(66, 69)

7. (Is, Are) your scissors sharp?
(92)

8. The sentence below is (simple, compound):
(75)

The pianist played well, but the singer's voice was flat.

9. The Grand Canyon is (sure, surely) beautiful.
(104)

10. Of the two hikers, Jill climbs the hill (faster, fastest).
(102)

11. For a–d, circle the correct definition. (1 point for each correct answer)

   (a) An (anarchy, enigma, estuary) is a riddle or mystery.
   (101)

   (b) Candid means (honest, dishonest, unethical).
   (102)

   (c) Parsimonious means (stingy, generous, extravagant).
   (104)

   (d) To (consecrate, desecrate, ameliorate) is to destroy.
   (105)

12. Add periods as needed in the sentence below.
(47, 50)

Ms Hoo left at two pm on the last day of school

13. Circle each letter that should be capitalized in the sentence below.
(42, 43)

the colorado river has carved the magnificent grand canyon in arizona.

14. For a–d, write the plural of each noun.
(16, 22)

   (a) coach _____   (b) library _____

   (c) gallon of milk _____   (d) mouse _____

15. Add punctuation marks as needed in the sentence below.

Do the sweet smelling flowers attract bees asks Andrew

16. Add a semicolon as needed in the sentence below.
(103)

Adventuresome folk can stay at Phantom Ranch in Grand Canyon however, it is only accessible by foot or mule.

17. Add a colon as needed in the sentence below.
(105)

The supply list includes these items tent, sleeping bag, lantern, and canteen.

18. Add quotation marks as needed in the sentence below.
(81)

Luis wrote a poem titled A Parsimonious Monarch.

19. Complete the four principal parts of the verb *forgive*.
(87)

<u>forgive</u>   (is) <u>   </u>   <u>   </u>   (has) <u>   </u>

  (1) present tense   (2) present participle   (3) past tense   (4) past participle

20. Circle the appositive phrase in the sentence below.
(58)

Amy baked a healthful snack, whole-grain muffins with raisins.

21. Underline the word that should be italicized in the sentence below.
(84)

I think that sentence contains a superfluous and.

22. Circle the adverb in the sentence below.
(100)

The forces of erosion are constantly changing the Grand Canyon's appearance.

23. Circle the subordinating conjunction in the sentence below.
(73, 74)

I shall hike up that mountain even though I am weary.

In the boxes provided, diagram each word of sentences 24 and 25.

24. Is the orca the whale with the
(45, 54) triangular fin?

> **24.**

25. Has the whale swum away?
(71, 91)

> **25.**

Circle the correct word(s) to complete sentences 1–10.

1. There wasn't (anybody, nobody) home.
(93)

2. Mr. Cuxil, (who, whom) we chose as our leader, has taught me valuable lessons.
(77)

3. Yesterday I was ill, but today I feel (good, well).
(96)

4. The clause below is (dependent, independent):
(73)

armadillos usually live alone

5. Each of the hikers (carry, carries) (their, his or her) own food and water.
(91)

6. Please tell Elle and (I, me) your secret.
(66, 69)

7. Mumps (is, are) a miserable disease.
(92)

8. The sentence below is (compound, complex, compound-complex):
(75, 110)

When my dog eats too much, his eyes bulge, and his stomach protrudes.

9. Josie was (real, really) frightened when she encountered a black bear.
(104)

10. (Between, Among) the many icebergs swam penguins and polar bears.
(107)

11. For a–d, circle the correct definition. (1 point for each correct answer)

(a) To (consecrate, ameliorate, beguile) is to mislead or deceive.
(106)

(b) To (beguile, digress, consecrate) is to depart from the main subject.
(107)

(c) Futile means (hopeless, effective, hopeful).
(108)

(d) (Dissension, Apathy, Digression) is lack of interest or concern.
(110)

12. Add periods as needed in the sentence below.
(47, 50)

Mr Cabrera wakes at six am to exercise

13. Circle each letter that should be capitalized in the sentence below.
(42, 43)

can you drive from olympia, washington, to juneau, alaska?

14. For a–d, write the plural of each noun.
(16, 22)

(a) toothbrush _____   (b) dictionary _____

(c) class president _____   (d) tooth _____

15. Add punctuation marks as needed in the sentence below.
(88)

Are the grizzlies hibernating asks Amelia

16. Add a semicolon and a comma as needed in the sentence below.
(103)

Most states have few grizzly bears however Alaska has many.

17. Add a colon as needed in the sentence below.
(105)

I remember one fact about grizzlies they are dangerous.

18. Add apostrophes as needed in the sentence below.
(108, 109)

That plumbers license wasnt valid, for it dated back to the year 73.

19. Complete the four principal parts of the verb *weave*.
(87)

weave	*(is)* _____	_____	*(has)* _____
(1) present tense	(2) present participle	(3) past tense	(4) past participle

20. Circle the indirect object in the sentence below.
(69)

Elle offered us a healthful snack of nuts and fruit.

21. Underline the word that should be italicized in the sentence below.
(84)

Squash can be either a noun or a verb.

22. Circle the adverb in the sentence below.
(95)

Two black bears are happily feasting on wild berries.

23. Circle the subordinating conjunction in the sentence below.
(73, 74)

My dog barks whenever she sees a bear.

In the boxes provided, diagram each word of sentences 24 and 25.

24. Is Fifi the poodle with the red
(45, 54) collar?

24.

25. Grizzlies can run incredibly fast.
(91, 101)

25.